WIRING DIAGRAMS PAL

Paul Rosenberg

The Professional's Choice!

Wiring Diagrams Pal is Volume Five of the Pal® Series of trade reference books designed and manufactured for contractors, maintenance personnel, service technicians and engineers.

Pal Publications
374 Circle of Progress
Pottstown, Pennsylvania 19464-3810

Toll-free: 1-800-246-2175
Fax: 1-800-396-1663

Email: info@palpublications.com
Website: www.palpublications.com

THIS BOOK BELONGS TO:

Name:_____

Company: _____

Title: _____

Department: _____

Company Address: _____

_____

_____

Company Phone: _____

Home Phone: _____

Date:_____

Pal Publications
374 Circle of Progress
Pottstown, PA 19464-3810

ISBN 0-9652171-4-0

08 07 06 05 04   5 4 3 2 1

Printed in the United States of America

A note to our customers from

We have manufactured this book to the highest quality standards possible. The cover is made of KIVAR®, a flexible, durable and water resistant material able to withstand the toughest on-the-job conditions. We also utilize the Otabind process which allows this book to lay flatter than traditional paperback books that tend to snap shut while in use.

Explanatory Notes

To make it easier for our readers, we have developed a standardized key to denote the various types of wires found in many of the diagrams. The first of such diagrams appears on page 1-19. Please refer to the wire key below when applicable.

<table>
<tr><td colspan="2" align="center">KEY FOR WIRES</td></tr>
<tr><td>Hot Wire ——————</td><td>Traveler Wire ——————</td></tr>
<tr><td>Neutral Wire – – – – – –</td><td>Ground Wire ——————</td></tr>
<tr><td>Switch Leg Wire — · — · — ·</td><td></td></tr>
</table>

PREFACE

Wiring diagrams are among the most useful information an electrician can have. Years ago I had an excellent book of wiring diagrams that I always tried to keep close at hand. Alas, somewhere along the line, I lost it and it is long out of print. So I was thrilled when Pal Publications suggested that we do a new one. I am very pleased that a good book of wiring diagrams is once again available to electricians.

This book contains all of the most essential wiring diagrams for most types of electrical work. Circuit wiring, grounding, transformer connections, motors and starters and lighting are all covered, plus a variety of specialties including several types of low voltage wiring diagrams. You will find more extensive coverage of motors and starters than other applications, simply because wiring diagrams are especially important for this type of work.

Naturally, there may be topics that were overlooked or are not covered in sufficient depth for some readers. I constantly monitor the industry and will update this book on a regular basis. I will attempt to include additional material suggested by readers and to modify the book to keep pace with new developments in the electrical trade.

Best wishes,
Paul Rosenberg

CONTENTS

CHAPTER 1 – *General Wiring, Lighting and Hazardous Locations* 1-1

CHAPTER 2 – *Low Voltage*. 2-1

CHAPTER 4 – *Motors and Controls* . . . 4-1

CHAPTER 6 – *Power Distribution* 6-1

CHAPTER 1
General Wiring, Lighting and Hazardous Locations

The central requirement for electrical wiring of all types is contained in section 110.12 of the National Electrical Code® (NEC) entitled "Mechanical Execution of Work." Electricians are required to install all electrical systems *in a neat and workmanlike manner.* Thus the Code specifies that not just materials are important, but that workmanship also is extremely important.

The wiring diagrams in this chapter cover a variety of installations including general electrical devices and operations, residential and lighting circuit diagrams and a number of diagrams covering hazardous location wiring.

Wiring in hazardous locations is subject to much more stringent requirements than other types and come with serious built-in dangers. Virtually all hazardous locations are covered in Articles 500 through 517 of the NEC and should be well understood by anyone wiring such locations. These areas are dangerous and have their own special requirements.

It is also important to remember that hazardous wiring is very expensive. Not only do the special types of equipment (explosion proof) cost more, but the amount of labor necessary to install the special equipment is very high. Use ingenuity in laying out wiring for hazardous locations. **Your goal is to locate as much of the wiring system as possible outside of the hazardous areas.**

Remember — all electrical installations in hazardous locations are inherently dangerous. Do not perform installations without carefully engineered layouts. If you do not have first-rate instructions, do not install the wiring! The diagrams shown in this chapter are given to assist in the installation process, not as a substitute for an engineered layout. Do not take chances.

OHM'S LAW DIAGRAM AND FORMULAS

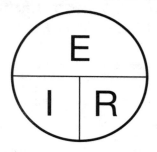

$E = I \times R$ Voltage = Current x Resistance
$I = E \div R$ Current = Voltage ÷ Resistance
$R = E \div I$ Resistance = Voltage ÷ Current

POWER DIAGRAM AND FORMULAS

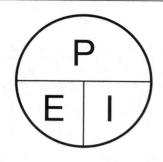

$I = P \div E$ Current = Power ÷ Voltage
$E = P \div I$ Voltage = Power ÷ Current
$P = I \times E$ Power = Current x Voltage

AC/DC FORMULAS FOR CALCULATING AMPS, HORSEPOWER, KILOWATTS AND kVA

To Find	Direct Current	Alternating Current		
		Single Phase	Two-Phase Four-Wire*	Three Phase
Amps when horsepower is known	$\dfrac{HP \times 746}{E \times E_{FF}}$	$\dfrac{HP \times 746}{E \times E_{FF} \times PF}$	$\dfrac{HP \times 746}{2 \times E \times E_{FF} \times PF}$	$\dfrac{HP \times 746}{1.73 \times E \times E_{FF} \times PF}$
Amps when kilowatts are known	$\dfrac{kW \times 1000}{E}$	$\dfrac{kW \times 1000}{E \times PF}$	$\dfrac{kW \times 1000}{2 \times E \times PF}$	$\dfrac{kW \times 1000}{1.73 \times E \times PF}$
Amps when kVA is known	—	$\dfrac{kVA \times 1000}{E}$	$\dfrac{kVA \times 1000}{2 \times E}$	$\dfrac{kVA \times 1000}{1.73 \times E}$
Kilowatts	$\dfrac{I \times E}{1000}$	$\dfrac{I \times E \times PF}{1000}$	$\dfrac{I \times E \times 2 \times PF}{1000}$	$\dfrac{I \times E \times 1.73 \times PF}{1000}$
Kilovolt-Amps (kVA)	—	$\dfrac{I \times E}{1000}$	$\dfrac{I \times E \times 2}{1000}$	$\dfrac{I \times E \times 1.73}{1000}$
Horsepower	$\dfrac{I \times E \times E_{FF}}{746}$	$\dfrac{I \times E \times E_{FF} \times PF}{746}$	$\dfrac{I \times E \times 2 \times E_{FF} \times PF}{746}$	$\dfrac{I \times E \times 1.73 \times E_{FF} \times PF}{746}$

I = Amps; E = Volts; E_{FF} = Efficiency; PF = Power Factor; kW = Kilowatts; kVA = Kilovolt Amps; HP = Horsepower

*For three wire, two phase circuits the current in the common conductor is 1.41 times the current in either of the other two conductors.

Power Factor = cos (Phase Angle)
Power Factor = True Power / Apparent Power
Power Factor = Watts / Volts x Amps

Power Factor = Resistance (in Ohms) / Impedance (in Ohms)
Efficiency = Output / Input

CIRCUIT CHARACTERISTICS

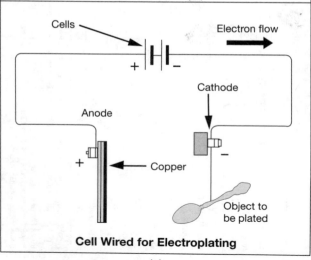

Dry Cell

Zinc

Paste

Carbon

Cell Wired for Electroplating

Cells

Electron flow

Cathode

Anode

Copper

Object to be plated

1-4

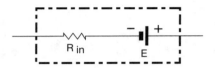

Equivalent Circuit

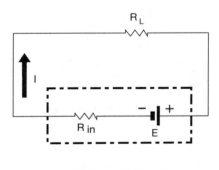

$$(I)\,R_{in} + (I)\,R_L = E$$

Equivalent Circuit Connected to Load Resistor

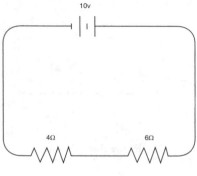

$$R_T = 10\Omega$$

Resistances in a Series DC Circuit

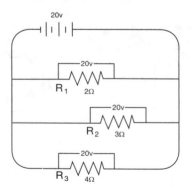

Parallel Circuit, Showing Voltage Drops

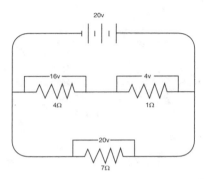

Voltages in a Series-Parallel Circuit

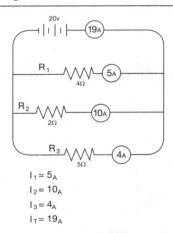

$I_1 = 5_A$
$I_2 = 10_A$
$I_3 = 4_A$
$I_T = 19_A$

Parallel Circuit, Showing Current Values

PERMISSIBLE BENDS

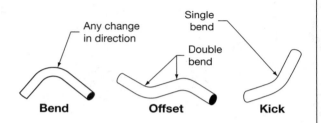

Any change in direction

Bend

Double bend

Offset

Single bend

Kick

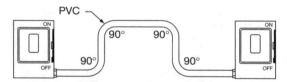

PVC

90°   90°

90°   90°

Total of 360° of bends is permitted.

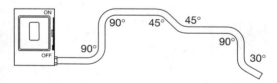

90°   45°   45°

90°   90°

30°

Over 360° of bends is not permitted.

BACK-TO-BACK BENDING

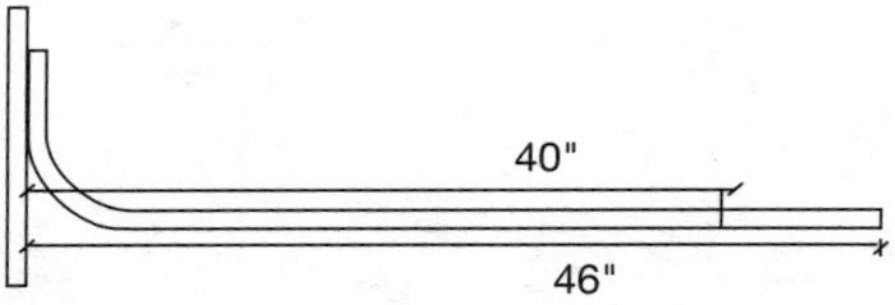

40"

46"

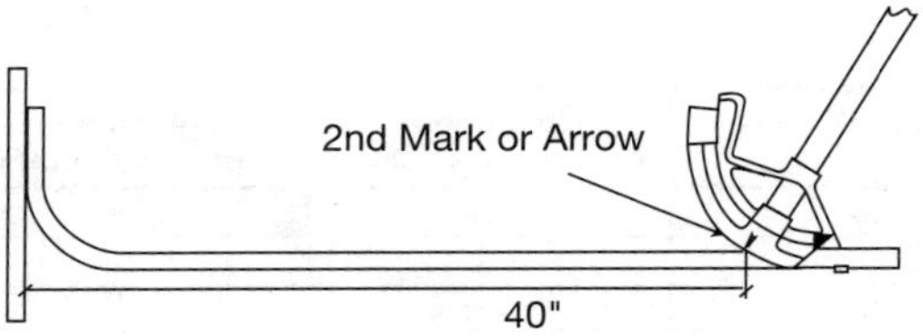

2nd Mark or Arrow

40"

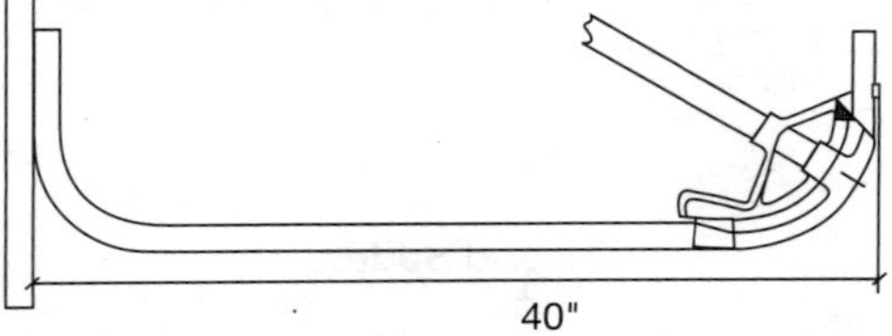

40"

OFFSET AND SADDLE BENDS

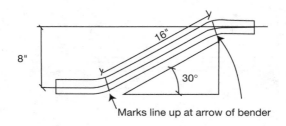

8"

16"

30°

Marks line up at arrow of bender

2-Bend Offset

Angle of Bends	Inches of run per inch of offset	Loss of conduit length per inch of offset
10°	5.76	1/16"
22.5°	2.6	3/16"
30°	2.0	1/4"
45°	1.414	3/8"
60°	1.15	1/2"

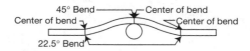

45° Bend — Center of bend
Center of bend — Center of bend
22.5° Bend

3-Bend Saddle

BENDING STUB-UPS

Conduit or EMT Size	Deduction from Mark or Arrow
½"	5"
¾"	6"
1"	8"

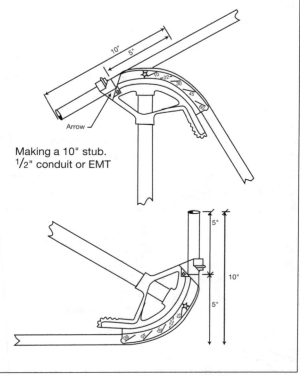

Making a 10" stub.
½" conduit or EMT

PULL AND CONNECTION POINTS

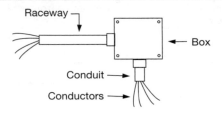

Raceway

Box

Conduit

Conductors

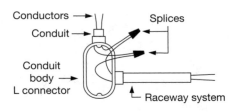

Conductors

Conduit

Splices

Conduit body
L connector

Raceway system

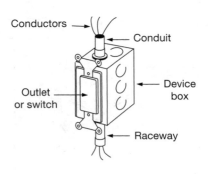

Conductors

Conduit

Outlet
or switch

Device
box

Raceway

WIRE-BENDING SPACE

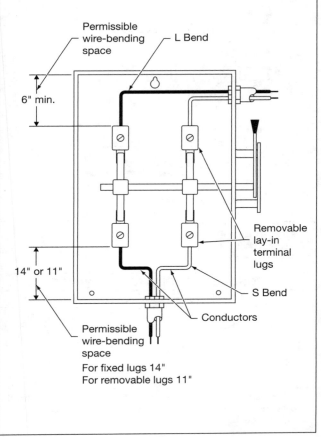

Permissible wire-bending space

L Bend

6" min.

Removable lay-in terminal lugs

S Bend

Conductors

14" or 11"

Permissible wire-bending space

For fixed lugs 14"
For removable lugs 11"

JUNCTION BOX CALCULATIONS

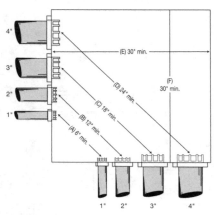

Distance (A) is 6 x 1" = 6" minimum
Distance (B) is 6 x 2" = 12" minimum
Distance (C) is 6 x 3" = 18" minimum
Distance (D) is 6 x 4" = 24" minimum
Distance (E) is (6 x 4") + 3" + 2" + 1" = 30" minimum
Distance (F) is (6 x 4") + 3" + 2" + 1" = 30" minimum

CONDUCTOR VOLUME ALLOWANCE

Wire Size (AWG)	Volume Each (In.³)	Formula
18	1.50	V = L . W . D
16	1.75	Volume =
14	2.00	Length times width
12	2.25	times depth =
10	2.50	cubic inches
8	3.00	
6	5.00	

To find box size needed, add up total volume for all wires to be used. Then use the volume formula; e.g., if total volume of all wires is 420 cu. in. – use an 8" x 10" x 6" box = 480 cu/ in.

BOX FILL

Max. Number of Conductors in Outlet, Device and Junction Boxes

Box Dimension in Inches Trade Size or Type	Min. Capacity (in.³)	Maximum Number of Conductors						
		No. 18	No. 16	No. 14	No. 12	No. 10	No. 8	No. 6
4 x 1¼ round or octagonal	12.5	8	7	6	5	5	5	2
4 x 1½ round or octagonal	15.5	10	8	7	6	6	5	3
4 x 2⅛ round or octagonal	21.5	14	12	10	9	8	7	4
4 x 1¼ square	18.0	12	10	9	8	7	6	3
4 x 1½ square	21.0	14	12	10	9	8	7	4
4 x 2⅛ square	30.3	20	17	15	13	12	10	6
4¹¹⁄₁₆ x 1¼ square	25.5	17	14	12	11	10	8	5
4¹¹⁄₁₆ x 1½ square	29.5	19	16	14	13	11	9	5
4¹¹⁄₁₆ x 2⅛ square	42.0	28	24	21	18	16	14	8
3 x 2 x 1½ device	7.5	5	4	3	3	3	2	1
3 x 2 x 2 device	10.0	6	5	5	4	4	3	2
3 x 2 x 2¼ device	10.5	7	6	5	4	4	3	2
3 x 2 x 2½ device	12.5	8	7	6	5	5	4	2
3 x 2 x 2¾ device	14.0	9	8	7	6	5	4	2
3 x 2 x 3½ device	18.0	12	10	9	8	7	6	3
4 x 2⅛ x 1½ device	10.3	6	5	5	4	4	3	2
4 x 2⅛ x 1⅞ device	13.0	8	7	6	5	5	4	2
4 x 2⅛ x 2⅛ device	14.5	9	8	7	6	5	4	2
3¾ x 2 x 2½ masonry box/gang	14.0	9	8	7	6	5	4	2
3¾ x 2 x 3½ masonry box/gang	21.0	14	12	10	9	8	7	2

Where one or more internal cable clamps are present in the box, a single volume allowance (conductor) shall be made based on the largest size conductor in the box.

ENCLOSURES IN WET LOCATIONS

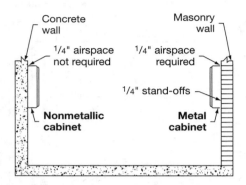

Both metal and nonmetallic enclosures installed in wet locations shall be weatherproof.

GROUNDED CONDUCTOR COLOR CODE

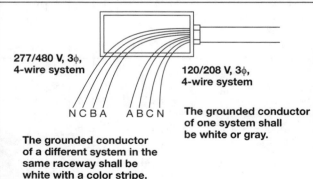

277/480 V, 3φ, 4-wire system

N C B A   A B C N

120/208 V, 3φ, 4-wire system

The grounded conductor of one system shall be white or gray.

The grounded conductor of a different system in the same raceway shall be white with a color stripe. (Do not use green as the color.)

GROUPED CONDUCTORS

**277/480 V, 3φ,
4-wire circuit**

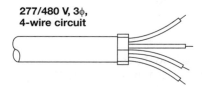

All phase conductors, grounded conductors, and equipment ground conductors shall be grouped together so as not to cause induction heating of metal raceways and enclosures.

PARALLELED CONDUCTORS

**Three parallel 4/0
THHN copper conductors
per phase**

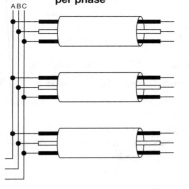

Requirements:

Same size
Same materials
Same length
Same insulation type
Same attachments

CONDUCTOR COLOR CODE

Grounded Conductor
- White
- Gray
- Three continuous white stripes

Ungrounded Conductor
- Any color other than white, gray, or green

Equipment Grounding Conductor
- Green with one or more yellow stripes
- Bare

POWER WIRING COLOR CODE

120/240 Volt		277/480 Volt	
Black	Phase 1	Brown	Phase 1
Red	Phase 2	Orange	Phase 2
Blue	Phase 3	Yellow	Phase 3
White or with 3 white stripes	Neutral	Gray or with 3 white stripes	Neutral
Green	Ground	Green with yellow stripe	Ground

POWER-TRANSFORMER COLOR CODE

Wire Color	Transformer Circuit Type
Black	If a transformer does not have a tapped primary, both leads are black.
Black	If a transformer does have a tapped primary, the black is the common lead.
Black and Yellow	Tap for a tapped primary.
Black and Red	End for a tapped primary.

BASIC GROUNDED CONDUCTOR RULES

Circuit breakers or switches shall not disconnect the grounded conductor of a circuit.

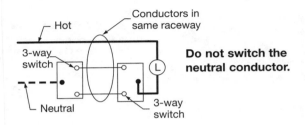

Hot

Conductors in same raceway

3-way switch

L

Do not switch the neutral conductor.

Neutral

3-way switch

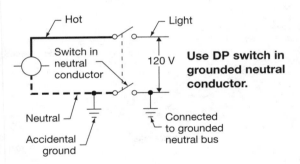

Hot

Light

Switch in neutral conductor

120 V

Use DP switch in grounded neutral conductor.

Neutral

Accidental ground

Connected to grounded neutral bus

Exception: A circuit breaker or switch may disconnect grounded circuit conductor if all circuit conductors are disconnected at the same time.

BASIC GROUNDED CONDUCTOR RULES *(cont.)*

Circuit breakers or switches shall not disconnect the grounded conductor of a circuit.

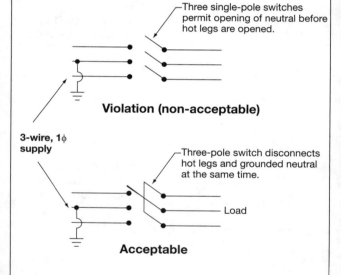

Three single-pole switches permit opening of neutral before hot legs are opened.

Violation (non-acceptable)

3-wire, 1φ supply

Three-pole switch disconnects hot legs and grounded neutral at the same time.

Load

Acceptable

Exception: A circuit breaker or switch may disconnect the grounded circuit conductor if it cannot be disconnected until all other ungrounded conductors have been disconnected.

MINIMUM SIZE CONDUCTORS FOR GROUNDING RACEWAY AND EQUIPMENT

Setting of automatic overcurrent devices in circuits ahead of equipment, conduit, etc., are not to exceed the amperage ratings below.	Size (AWG or kcmil)	
	Copper	Aluminum or copper-clad aluminum
15	14 AWG	12 AWG
20	12	10
30	10	8
40	10	8
60	10	8
100	8	6
200	6	4
300	4	2
400	3	1
500	2	1/0
600	1	2/0
800	1/0	3/0
1000	2/0	4/0
1200	3/0	250 kcmil
1600	4/0	350
2000	250 kcmil	400
2500	350	600
3000	400	600
4000	500	800
5000	700	1200
6000	800	1200

UNDERGROUND INSTALLATION REQUIREMENTS

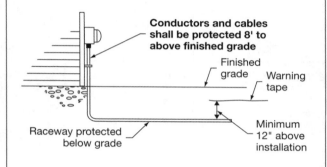

Conductors and cables shall be protected 8' to above finished grade

Finished grade

Warning tape

Raceway protected below grade

Minimum 12" above installation

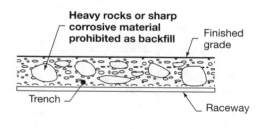

Heavy rocks or sharp corrosive material prohibited as backfill

Finished grade

Trench

Raceway

UNDERGROUND
INSTALLATION REQUIREMENTS *(cont.)*

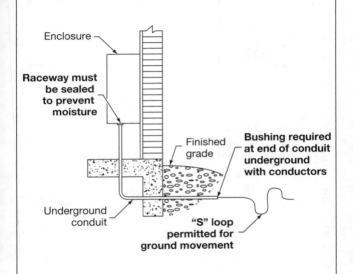

Enclosure

Raceway must be sealed to prevent moisture

Finished grade

Bushing required at end of conduit underground with conductors

Underground conduit

"S" loop permitted for ground movement

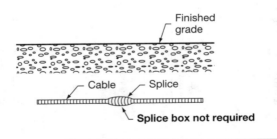

Finished grade

Cable — Splice

Splice box not required

MINIMUM COVER REQUIREMENTS FOR UNDERGROUND INSTALLATIONS

Location of circuit or wiring method	Type of circuit or wiring method (0 to 600 Volts, nominal)				
	Direct burial cables or conductors	Rigid metal conduit or intermediate metal conduit	Nonmetallic raceways listed for direct burial without concrete encasement or other approved raceways	Residential branch circuits rated 120 V or less with GFCI protection and maximum over-current protection of 20 amperes	Circuits for control of irrigation and landscape lighting limited to not more than 30 V and installed with type UF or in other identified cable or raceway
All locations not specified in these charts	24"	6"	18"	12"	6"
In trench below 2" thick concrete or equivalent	18"	6"	12"	6"	6"
Under buildings	(In raceway only)	—	—	— (In raceway only)	— (In raceway only)
Under minimum of 4" thick concrete exterior slab with no traffic and slab extending no less than 6 inches beyond the installation	18"	4"	4"	6" (Direct burial) 4" (In raceway)	6" (Direct burial) 4" (In raceway)
Under alleys, highways, roads, driveways, streets, and parking lots	24"	24"	24"	24"	24"

MINIMUM COVER REQUIREMENTS FOR UNDERGROUND INSTALLATIONS (cont.)

Type of circuit or wiring method (0 to 600 Volts, nominal)

Location of circuit or wiring method	Direct burial cables or conductors	Rigid metal conduit or intermediate metal conduit	Nonmetallic raceways listed for direct burial without concrete encasement or other approved raceways	Residential branch circuits rated 120 V or less with GFCI protection and maximum over-current protection of 20 amperes	Circuits for control of irrigation and landscape lighting limited to not more than 30 V and installed with type UF or in other identified cable or raceway
Under family dwelling driveways. Outdoor parking areas used for dwelling-related purposes only	18"	18"	18"	12"	18"
In or under airport runways including areas where the public is prohibited	18"	18"	18"	18"	18"

Notes: Cover is defined as the shortest distance between a point on the top service of any direct-buried conductor, cable, conduit or other raceway and the top surface of finished grade, concrete, etc.

Raceways approved for burial only where concrete encased shall require a 2" concrete envelope.

Lesser depths are permitted where cables/conductors rise for terminations, splices or equipment.

Where solid rock prevents compliance with the cover depths specified in this table, the wiring must be installed in raceways permitted for direct burial. The raceways shall be covered by a minimum of 2" of concrete extending down to the solid rock.

FAMILY ROOM RECEPTACLE OUTLET SPACING

(A) No point along floor line shall be more than 6' from a receptacle outlet.

(B) All wall spaces 2' or larger shall have a receptacle outlet.

12'

12'

6'

6'

(A)

(B) French doors

2'

Sliding doors

18"

Receptacle not required

6'

6'

12'

1-26

FAMILY ROOM WITH SPLIT-WIRED RECEPTACLES AND SWITCHED CIRCUIT

A split-wired receptacle has the tab between the brass (hot) terminals removed but silver (neutral) terminals remain intact. This provides either a switched circuit or two separate circuits at the same receptacle outlet.

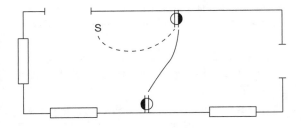

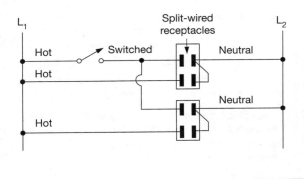

COUNTERTOP RECEPTACLE OUTLET SPACING

The following pertains to receptacle outlets for counterspaces in kitchens, dining rooms and bar areas of dwelling units.

- A receptacle outlet shall be installed for all countertops that are 12" wide or larger.

- There shall be no point along the wall greater than 24" from a receptacle outlet. This is due to change in standards for kitchen countertop appliances such as blenders and food processors. There is a requirement of a 2' cord and plug for any appliance used on top of counters.

- For each island countertop that is 24" x 12" or larger, there shall be at least one receptacle outlet installed.

- For each peninsula countertop space that measures 24" x 12" or larger, there shall be at least one receptacle outlet installed. This measurement is from the connection point between countertops.

- Countertops separated by appliances or sinks are considered separate spaces and require receptacle outlets per the above requirement.

- The location of outlets shall not be more than 18" above the surface of the countertop and shall not be installed in a face-up position on the countertop.

- Receptacle outlets must be installed 12" or less below the countertop. This is for the physically disabled or when construction prevents practical mounting above the countertop.

COUNTERTOP RECEPTACLE OUTLET SPACING (cont.)

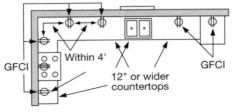

Maximum 18"

GFCI   GFCI

24" or greater

Minimum one outlet

GFCI

ISLAND

12" or greater

12" or less below countertop

12" or greater

Minimum one outlet

Countertop extension maximum 6"

24" or greater

GFCI

Within 4'

GFCI

12" or wider countertops

KITCHEN RECEPTACLES

All receptacles must be on small appliance circuits and GFCI protection is required for all receptacles serving kitchen countertops and countertop surfaces.

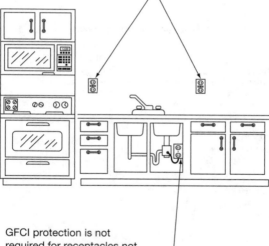

GFCI protection is not required for receptacles not serving countertop surfaces or dedicated appliances such as a garbage disposal.

BATHROOM RECEPTACLES

At least one wall receptacle outlet shall be installed within 36" of outside edge of each basin and on a wall adjacent to basin location.

←36"→　　　←36"→

All GFCI-protected receptacles shall be supplied by at least one 20 amp circuit with no other type of outlets on the circuit.

All bathroom receptacles in dwelling units are required to be GFCI-protected.

WET BAR RECEPTACLES

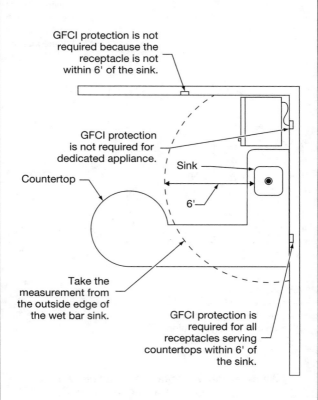

GFCI protection is not required because the receptacle is not within 6' of the sink.

GFCI protection is not required for dedicated appliance.

Sink

Countertop

6'

Take the measurement from the outside edge of the wet bar sink.

GFCI protection is required for all receptacles serving countertops within 6' of the sink.

CRAWL SPACE RECEPTACLES

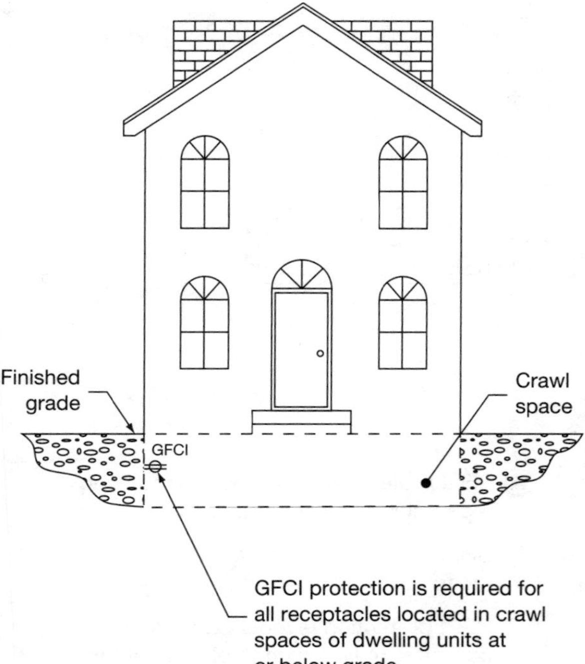

Finished grade

Crawl space

GFCI

GFCI protection is required for all receptacles located in crawl spaces of dwelling units at or below grade.

UNFINISHED BASEMENT RECEPTACLES

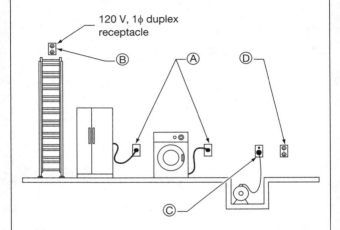

120 V, 1φ duplex receptacle

Ⓐ GFCI protection is not required for single receptacles powering dedicated appliances.

Ⓑ GFCI protection is not required for any receptacles that are not readily accessible.

Ⓒ GFCI protection is required for sump pumps supplied from duplex receptacles.

Ⓓ GFCI protection is required for all other duplex receptacles.

GARAGE/SHOP RECEPTACLES

Dedicated appliance

GFCI protection is required for all duplex receptacles in a garage not intended as a living space.

GFCI protection is not required for single dedicated receptacles.

Grade level

Accessory buildings at or below grade not intended as living space require GFCI protection on all duplex receptacles.

OUTDOOR RECEPTACLES

GFCI protection is not required
for receptacles utilizing snow and
ice melting equipment and are
not readily accessible.

A GFCI
receptacle is
required for all
outdoor
lighting.

A GFCI
receptacle is
required
regardless of
height except
as noted
above.

GFCI protection
is required on all
outdoor receptacles
on dwelling units.

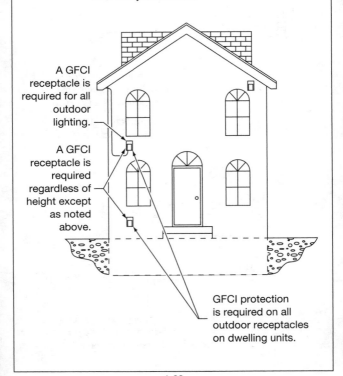

ISOLATED GROUND RECEPTACLE

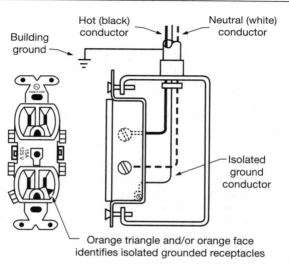

Hot (black) conductor

Neutral (white) conductor

Building ground

Isolated ground conductor

Orange triangle and/or orange face identifies isolated grounded receptacles

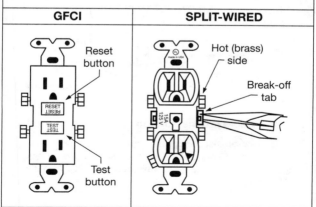

GFCI

Reset button

Test button

SPLIT-WIRED

Hot (brass) side

Break-off tab

GFCI WIRING DIAGRAMS

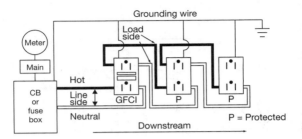

Feed-Thru Installation

To protect the entire branch circuit, the GFCI must be the first receptacle from the circuit breaker or fuse box. Receptacles on the circuit downstream from the GFCI will also be protected.

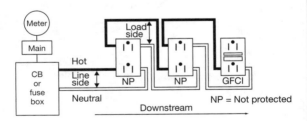

Non-Feed-Thru Installation on a 2-Wire Circuit

Terminal protection can be achieved on a multi-outlet circuit by connecting the hot and neutral line conductors to the corresponding line side terminals of the GFCI. Only the GFCI receptacle will be protected.

WIRING DIAGRAMS FOR NEMA CONFIGURATIONS

2-Pole 2-Wire Non-Grounding

125 V

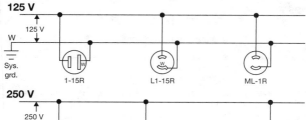

250 V

3-Pole 3-Wire Non-Grounding

125/250 V

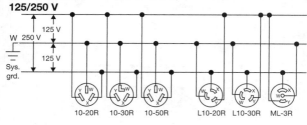

3φ 250 V

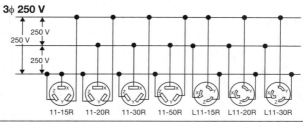

WIRING DIAGRAMS FOR
NEMA CONFIGURATIONS *(cont.)*

2-Pole 3-Wire Grounding

125 V

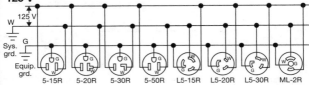

5-15R 5-20R 5-30R 5-50R L5-15R L5-20R L5-30R ML-2R

250 V

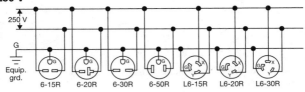

6-15R 6-20R 6-30R 6-50R L6-15R L6-20R L6-30R

277 VAC

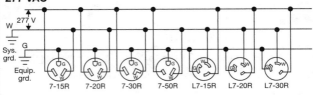

7-15R 7-20R 7-30R 7-50R L7-15R L7-20R L7-30R

480 VAC

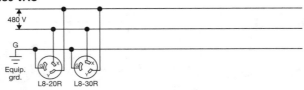

L8-20R L8-30R

WIRING DIAGRAMS FOR
NEMA CONFIGURATIONS *(cont.)*

3-Pole 4-Wire Grounding
125 V/250 V

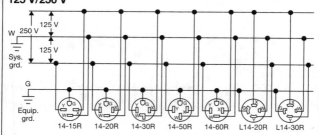

W 250 V

125 V
125 V

Sys. grd.

G

Equip. grd.

14-15R 14-20R 14-30R 14-50R 14-60R L14-20R L14-30R

3φ 250 V

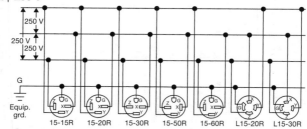

250 V

250 V
250 V

G

Equip. grd.

15-15R 15-20R 15-30R 15-50R 15-60R L15-20R L15-30R

3φ 480 V

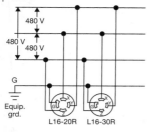

480 V

480 V
480 V

G

Equip. grd.

L16-20R L16-30R

3φ 600 V

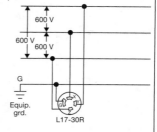

600 V

600 V
600 V

G

Equip. grd.

L17-30R

1-41

WIRING DIAGRAMS FOR
NEMA CONFIGURATIONS *(cont.)*

4-Pole 4-Wire Non-Grounding
3φ Wye 120 V/208 V

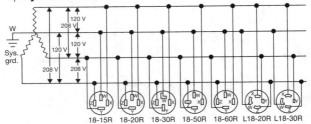

18-15R 18-20R 18-30R 18-50R 18-60R L18-20R L18-30R

3φ Wye 277 V/480 V

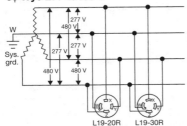

L19-20R L19-30R

3φ Wye 347 V/600 V

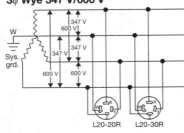

L20-20R L20-30R

WIRING DIAGRAMS FOR
NEMA CONFIGURATIONS *(cont.)*

4-Pole 5-Wire Grounding
3φ Wye 120 V/208 V

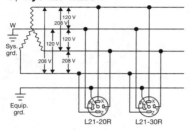

3φ Wye 277 V/480 V

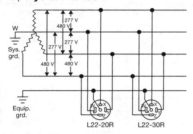

3φ Wye 347 V/600 V

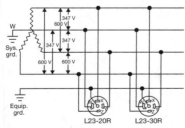

WIRING DIAGRAMS FOR SWITCHES

AC Switches

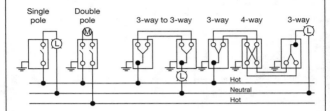

Pilot Light and Lighted Toggle Switches

Single Pole Pilot Light Switch
Toggle glows when light is on.

Single Pole Lighted Toggle Switch
Toggle glows when switch is off.

Double Pole Pilot Light Switch
Toggle glows when switch is on.

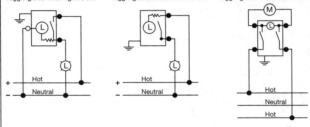

3-Way Lighted Toggle Switch

3-Way Pilot Lighted Toggle Switch

WIRING DIAGRAM OF SPLIT-WIRED RECEPTACLES AND SWITCHED CIRCUIT

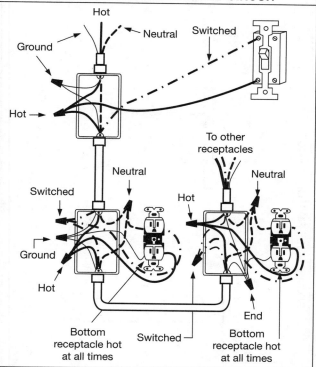

Hot

Neutral

Switched

Ground

Hot

To other receptacles

Neutral

Neutral

Switched

Hot

Ground

Hot

Bottom receptacle hot at all times

Switched

End

Bottom receptacle hot at all times

KEY FOR WIRES

Hot Wire ——————— Traveler Wire ———————

Neutral Wire — — — — — — Ground Wire ———————

Switch Leg Wire —·—·—·—

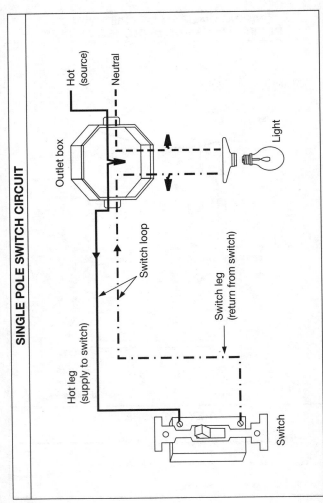

SINGLE POLE SWITCH CIRCUIT

Hot (source)

Neutral

Outlet box

Light

Switch loop

Switch leg (return from switch)

Hot leg (supply to switch)

Switch

CUSTOMER CARE SURVEY – WIN A FREE 27" COLOR TV   WD04

Form must be fully completed with company information. Contest void in states where prohibited or regulated by law.

Name _____ Title _____

Company Name _____ Tel _____

Company Address _____ Fax _____

City _____ State _____ Zip _____ Email _____

WHICH ONE BEST DESCRIBES YOUR PRIMARY ACTIVITY?
☐ Manufacturing/Processing (products) ☐ Commercial/Institutional (service) ☐ Construction/Contracting

WHAT PRIMARY PRODUCT TYPE?
☐ Oil/Gas/Mining
☐ Food/Kindred
☐ Textile/Apparel
☐ Lumber/Wood
☐ Printing/Publishing
☐ Chemicals & Related
☐ Electrical/Electronics
☐ Fab./Primary Metals
☐ Machinery/Equipment

☐ Plastic/Rubber
☐ Stone/Glass/Clay
☐ Transportation

TYPE OF SERVICE?
☐ Transportation/Shipping
☐ Warehousing
☐ Utilities
☐ Tel./Data Com.
☐ Wholesale Distribution
☐ Banking/Financial

☐ Health/Medical
☐ Educational/Training
☐ Engineering
☐ Govt./Public Ad.
☐ Advertising/Media
☐ Computer/Internet

TYPE OF CONTRACTING?
☐ General/Framing
☐ Excavation
☐ Concrete/Masonry

☐ Steel Erection/Mech.
☐ Electrical
☐ Cabling/Fiber Optics
☐ Plumbing
☐ HVAC & Refrig.

COMPANY SIZE
☐ 1-19   ☐ 100-249
☐ 20-49   ☐ 250-499
☐ 50-99   ☐ 500 +

WHICH OF THE FOLLOWING PRODUCT TYPES DO YOU RECOMMEND, SPECIFY OR BUY?
☐ Electrical/Electronics
☐ Plant Maint. (MRO)

☐ Safety/Security/Health
☐ Hazmat Control

☐ Piping/Pumps/Valves
☐ HVAC & Refrig.

☐ Mach. & Equipment
☐ Computers/Software
☐ Data Com./Fiber Optics

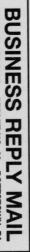

SINGLE POLE OPERATING A LIGHT WITH ADDITIONAL INDEPENDENT RECEPTACLE

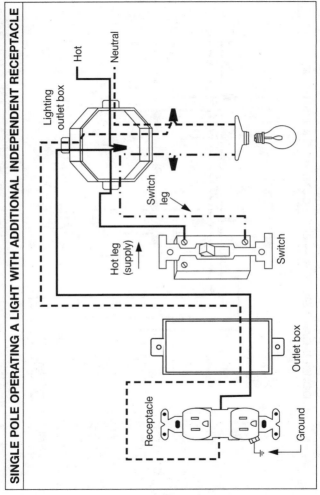

Hot

Neutral

Lighting outlet box

Switch leg

Hot leg (supply)

Switch

Outlet box

Receptacle

Ground

1-47

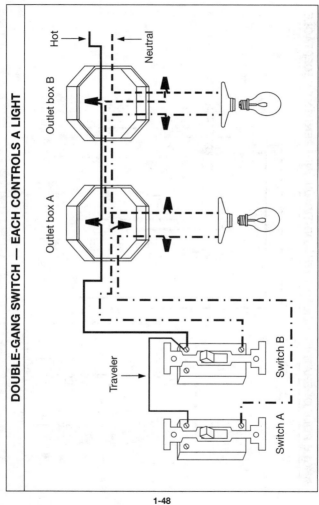

DOUBLE-GANG SWITCH — EACH CONTROLS A LIGHT

Hot

Neutral

Outlet box B

Outlet box A

Traveler

Switch B

Switch A

1-48

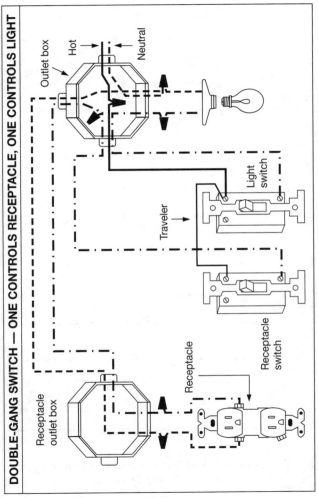

DOUBLE-GANG SWITCH — ONE CONTROLS RECEPTACLE, ONE CONTROLS LIGHT

Hot

Neutral

Outlet box

Light switch

Traveler

Receptacle switch

Receptacle outlet box

Receptacle

1-49

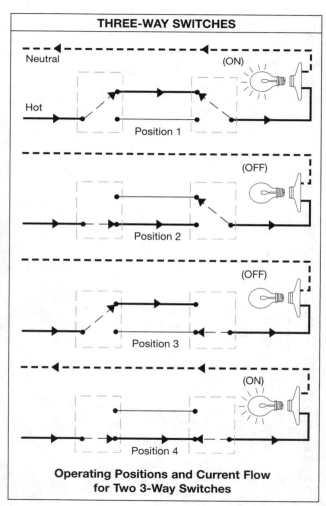

THREE-WAY SWITCHES

Neutral

(ON)

Hot

Position 1

(OFF)

Position 2

(OFF)

Position 3

(ON)

Position 4

**Operating Positions and Current Flow
for Two 3-Way Switches**

THREE- AND FOUR-WAY SWITCHES

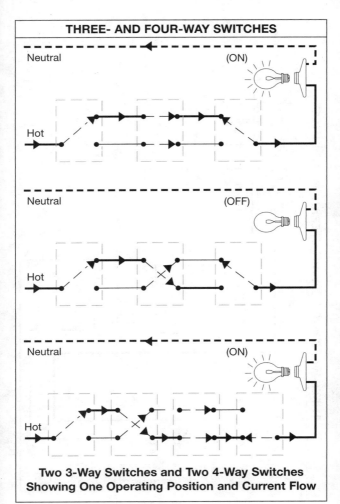

**Two 3-Way Switches and Two 4-Way Switches
Showing One Operating Position and Current Flow**

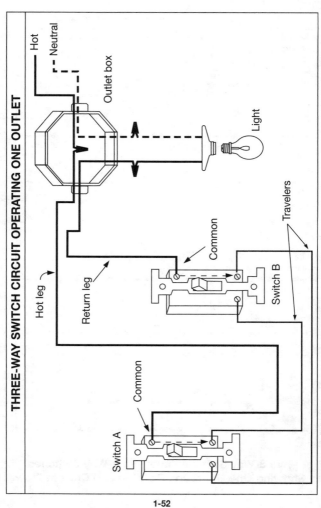

THREE-WAY SWITCH CIRCUIT OPERATING ONE OUTLET

Hot
Neutral
Outlet box
Light
Common
Switch B
Travelers
Hot leg
Return leg
Common
Switch A

1-52

THREE-WAY SWITCH CIRCUIT OPERATING ONE OUTLET FROM TWO LOCATIONS

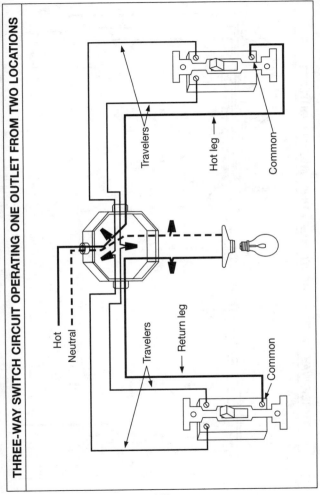

Travelers

Common

Hot leg

Hot

Neutral

Travelers

Return leg

Common

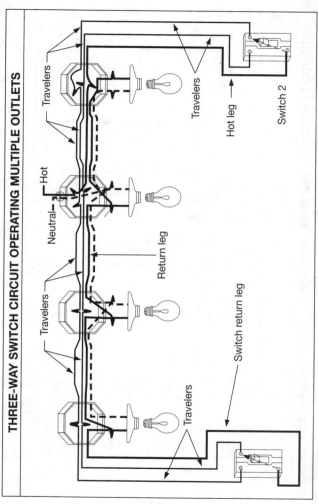

THREE-WAY SWITCH CIRCUIT OPERATING MULTIPLE OUTLETS

Travelers

Travelers

Travelers

Switch 2

Hot leg

Hot

Neutral

Return leg

Travelers

Switch return leg

Travelers

1-54

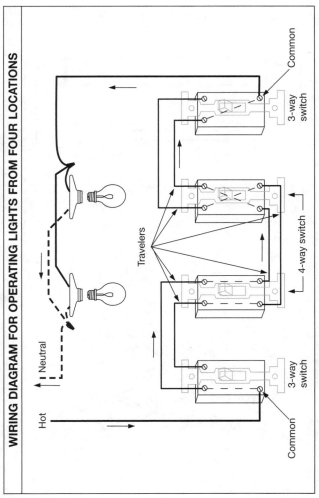

WIRING DIAGRAM FOR OPERATING LIGHTS FROM FOUR LOCATIONS

Common

3-way switch

4-way switch

Travelers

3-way switch

Common

Neutral

Hot

PREHEAT CIRCUITS

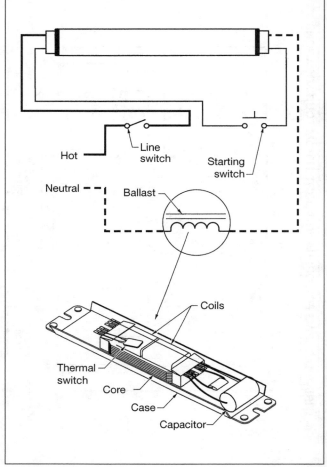

1-56

RAPID-START CIRCUITS

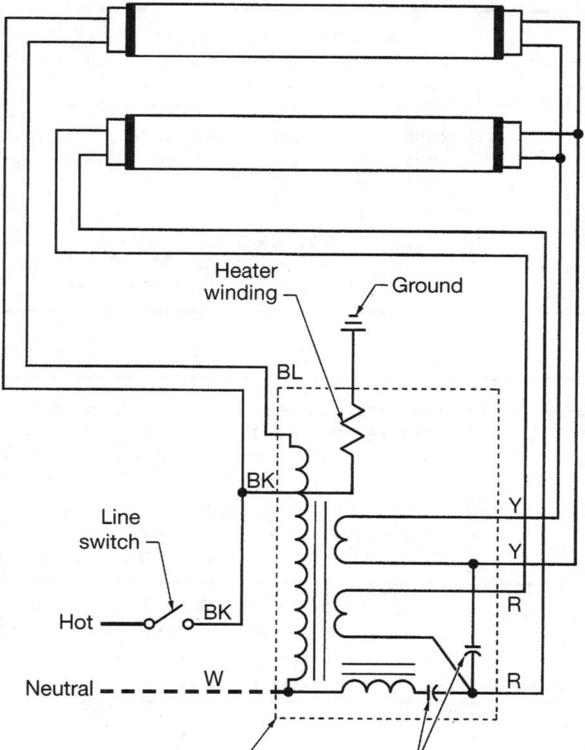

Heater winding

Ground

BL

BK

Line switch

Hot

BK

Neutral

W

Y

Y

R

R

Ballast

Capacitors

1-57

CLASSIFICATIONS OF HAZARDOUS LOCATIONS

Classes	Likelihood that a flammable or combustible concentration is present.
I	Sufficient quantities of flammable gases and vapors present in air to cause an explosion or ignite hazardous materials.
II	Sufficient quantities of combustible dust are present in air to cause an explosion or ignite hazardous materials.
III	Easily-ignitable fibers or flyings are present in air, but not in a sufficient quantity to cause an explosion or ignite hazardous materials.

Divisions	Location containing hazardous substances.
1	Hazardous location in which hazardous substance is **normally present** in air in sufficient quantities to cause an explosion or ignite hazardous materials.
2	Hazardous location in which hazardous substance is **not normally present** in air in sufficient quantities to cause an explosion or ignite hazardous materials.

Groups	Atmosphere containing flammable gases or vapors or combustible dust.	
Class I	**Class II**	**Class III**
A	E	
B	F	none
C	G	
D		

STANDARD AND OPTIONAL
HAZARDOUS LOCATION SYSTEMS

Standard System

Class I — **Flammable Gases or Vapors**
Division 1 — Normally Present in Air
Division 2 — Not Normally Present in Air

Class II — **Combustible Dust**
Division 1 — Normally Present in Air
Division 2 — Not Normally Present in Air

Class III — **Ignitable Fibers or Flyings**
Division 1 — Normally Present in Air
Division 2 — Not Normally Present in Air

Optional System*

Zone 0 — Flammable Gases or Vapors are Present Continuously or for Long Periods of Time

Zone 1 — Flammable Gases or Vapors are Likely to Exist Under Normal Operating Conditions or Exist Frequently

Zone 2 — Flammable Gases or Vapors are not Normally Present or are Present for Short Periods of Time

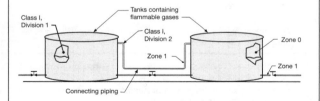

Class I, Division 1 — Tanks containing flammable gases — Class I, Division 2 — Zone 0 — Zone 1 — Zone 2 — Connecting piping

*The Optional Classification System as well as Area Classifications, Wiring Methods, and Equipment Selection can only be utilized under supervision of a qualified registered professional engineer.

DIVISION 1 EXAMPLES

Class I

- Spray booth interiors.
- Areas adjacent to spraying or painting operations using volatile flammable solvents.
- Open tanks or vats of volatile flammable liquids.
- Drying or evaporation rooms for flammable solvents.
- Areas where fats and oil extraction equipment using flammable solvents are operated.
- Cleaning and dyeing plant rooms that use flammable liquids.
- Gas generator rooms.
- Pump rooms for flammable gases or volatile flammable liquids that do not contain adequate ventilation.
- Refrigeration or freezer interiors that store flammable materials.
- All other locations where sufficient ignitable quantities of flammable gases or vapors are likely to occur during routine operations.

Class II

- Grain and grain products.
- Pulverized sugar and cocoa.
- Dried egg and milk powders.
- Pulverized spices.
- Starch and pastes.
- Potato and woodflour.
- Oil meal from beans and seeds.
- Dried hay.
- Any other organic materials that may produce combustible dusts during their use or handling.

Class III

- Portions of rayon, cotton, or other textile mills.
- Manufacturing and processing plants for combustible fibers, cotton gins, and cotton seed mills.
- Flax processing plants.
- Clothing manufacturing plants.
- Woodworking plants.
- Other establishments involving similar hazardous processes or conditions.

EXPLOSIONPROOF REDUCERS

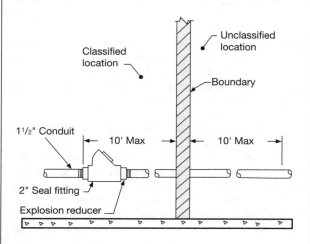

Approved Explosionproof Reducers are only fittings permitted between seal fitting and point of entrance to boundary of the classified location. Conduit seal fittings are installed at hazardous location boundaries to prevent communication of the hazardous substance between the classified and unclassified areas.

CONDUIT SEALS

A *conduit seal* is a fitting which is inserted into runs of conduit to isolate certain electrical apparatus from atmospheric hazards. Conduit seals contain provisions for pouring a sealing compound into the fitting to accomplish the isolation.

The purpose of the conduit seal is to minimize the passage of gases and vapors and to prevent the passage of flames from one area of an electrical installation to another. Seal fittings can be designed for either vertical or horizontal mounting in the conduit system and in male and female configurations. In some cases, the seal fittings may be mounted in any position.

Conduit seals shall be installed in accordance with the manufacturer's instructions which may contain location specifications. For example, the preferred side of a classified area boundary where the seal shall be installed may be given. In addition, the sealing compound also contains installation instructions and directions for making the seal.

Conduit seals shall be provided for each conduit entry into an explosionproof enclosure that contains apparatus which may produce sparks, arcs, or excessive temperatures. Conduit seals shall also be provided for each conduit entry into an explosionproof enclosure where the entry is 2" or larger and the enclosure contains terminals, splices, or taps. The conduit seals shall be located within 18" from the enclosure. Only explosionproof fittings and conduit bodies are permitted to be installed between the conduit seal and the explosionproof enclosure.

DISPENSING EQUIPMENT CONDUIT SEALS

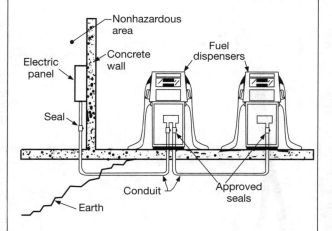

Gasoline and service station dispensing equipment conduit seals shall be the first fitting installed after the conduit leaves the concrete or the earth.

FUEL DISPENSER HAZARDOUS AREAS

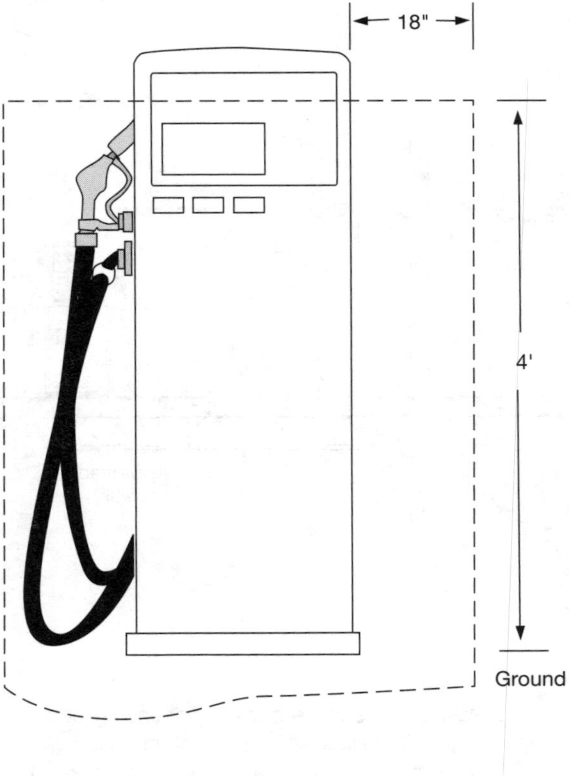

18"

4'

Ground

SERVICE STATION HAZARDOUS AREAS

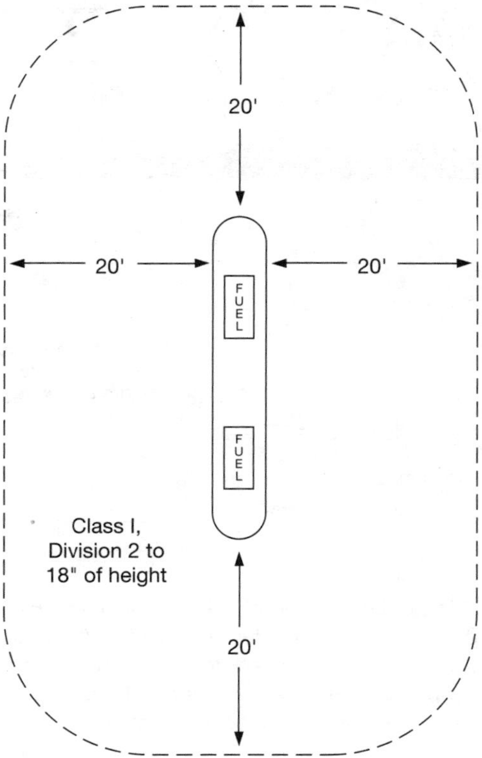

20'

20' ← → 20'

FUEL

FUEL

Class I,
Division 2 to
18" of height

20'

DISPENSING EQUIPMENT DISCONNECTING MEANS

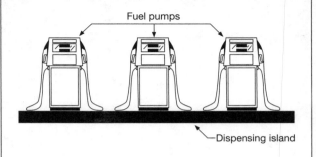

Fuel pumps

Dispensing island

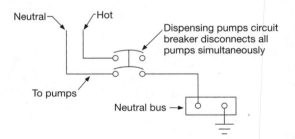

Neutral

Hot

Dispensing pumps circuit breaker disconnects all pumps simultaneously

To pumps

Neutral bus

In addition to the circuit ungrounded conductors, the grounded conductor (neutral) shall be disconnected from the source of supply if it supplies or passes through dispensing equipment in service stations.

HAZARDOUS LOCATIONS — COMMERCIAL GARAGES

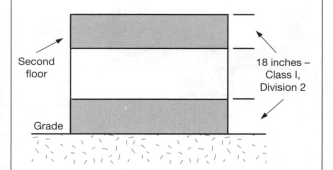

Second floor

18 inches – Class I, Division 2

Grade

Hazardous Areas of Commercial Garages Above Grade Level

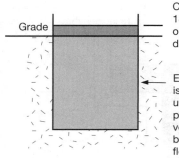

Grade

Class I, Division 2, 18 inches above grade or 18 inches above door opening.

Entire area below grade is Class I, Division 2 unless adequate and positive-pressure ventilated and judged to be 18 inches above the floor by the inspector.

Hazardous Areas of Commercial Garages Below Grade Level

HAZARDOUS LOCATIONS — PITS

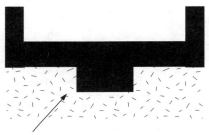

Class I, Division 2, 18 inches above grade or door opening.

A pit is Class I, Division 2, but may be judged Class I, Division 1 by the inspector if not properly ventilated.

Hazardous Areas and Classification of Pits or Depressions in Garage Floors

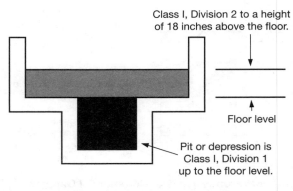

Class I, Division 2 to a height of 18 inches above the floor.

Floor level

Pit or depression is Class I, Division 1 up to the floor level.

Hazardous Areas in Aircraft Hangars

HAZARDOUS LOCATIONS — STORAGE TANKS

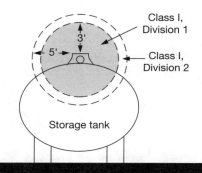

Class I, Division 1

Class I, Division 2

3'

5'

Storage tank

Classification Around Vents

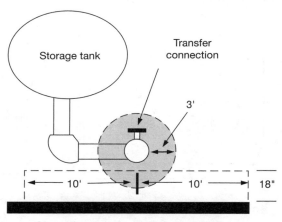

Storage tank

Transfer connection

3'

10'

10'

18"

Classification Around Bottom Filler

1-69

HAZARDOUS LOCATIONS — VERTICAL TANKS

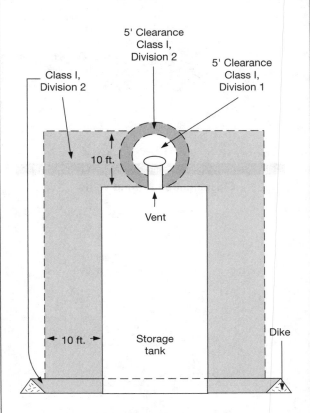

Classification Around Vertical Tank

HAZARDOUS LOCATIONS — VENT PIPES

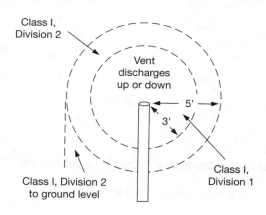

Class I, Division 2

Vent discharges up or down

5'

3'

Class I, Division 1

Class I, Division 2 to ground level

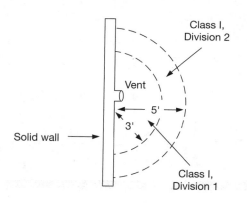

Class I, Division 2

Vent

5'

3'

Solid wall

Class I, Division 1

Vent Pipe Hazardous Areas

HAZARDOUS LOCATIONS — VENTILATION

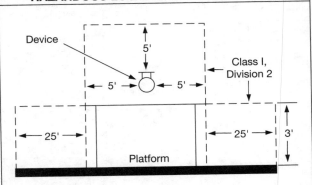

Adequately Ventilated Indoor Areas

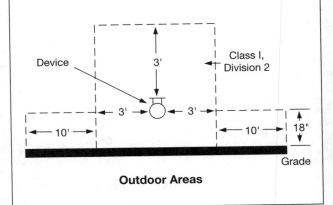

Outdoor Areas

CHAPTER 2
Low Voltage

Low-voltage (electronic) wiring has been part of the electrical trades since they began. Bells, chimes, control circuits, alarm circuitry and other systems are as old as power wiring. In recent years, a large number of electronic and microprocessor devices have become very common. The basic laws that govern electricity (i.e., ohm's law) govern electronics. The main difference is the amount of power being used.

The names of the devices are especially intimidating: Zener diodes, field-effect transistors, PNP junctions, etc. Yet these are no more than fancy names for such things as automatic switches and are not difficult to understand and use once you cut through the mystique surrounding them.

The basic rules of working with electrical components also apply to electronic devices. Handle with care and make sure that you use parts at or below their rated voltage and wattage. Failure to keep these components within their limits will usually result in a prompt blowout.

Most electronic parts are durable, but pay extra attention to the temperatures at which they are stored or operated. High temperatures can have a deteriorating effect. Also beware of installing parts with pins. Take extra care not to bend the pins and insert them straight into place. Do not twist and turn them—they cannot take the stress.

LOW-VOLTAGE CIRCUITS

Low-voltage remote switching systems allow greater flexibility and safety in controlling electric devices such as lights and motors. In remote control wiring systems, relays perform the actual switching of the current. The relays are controlled by small switches that operate on low voltage (such as 24 V) which is stepped down by a transformer.

The wiring diagram below demonstrates how a low-voltage control circuit operates. A switch with an iron knob is moved into the ON position by energizing a coil with low voltage from a battery by closing the push button switch. Low-voltage control switches like the push button are momentary contact switches, meaning that the current only flows for the length of time the switch is pressed. Therefore, the iron knob switch in the example will remain in the ON position so that it is no longer necessary to energize the coil.

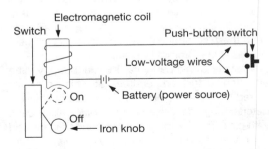

Principle of Low-Voltage Control

To further enhance our example, let us add an additional coil and wire to the circuit, allowing for an OFF position. The diagram below illustrates that when the lower coil is energized, the iron knob switch will be drawn down to the coil into an OFF position. A battery still remains as the power source.

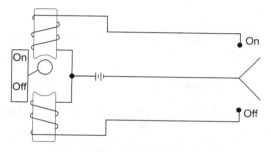

**Two Position Switching by
Three-Wire Low-Voltage Control**

By using a transformer, we can tap into a larger power source such as 120 volt AC. Also, the coils can be combined into one switch with a center tap resulting in a reduction in size.

The diagram on the following page shows a circuit utilizing 120 volt AC current in two ways, powering a light and powering a low-voltage circuit to operate the light using a transformer to step down the voltage.

By connecting one side of the step-down transformer to the center top of the coil, each half of the coil can be energized by the push button switch. If the push button is pressed off (as shown by the arrow), the left-hand side of the coil is energized, moving the plunger to the left and opening the circuit, causing the light to be off.

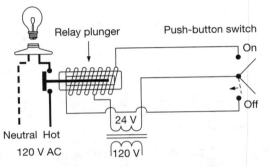

The diagram below illustrates how a basic remote control circuit with one switch, one relay and a fuse will look in the field.

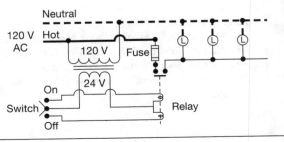

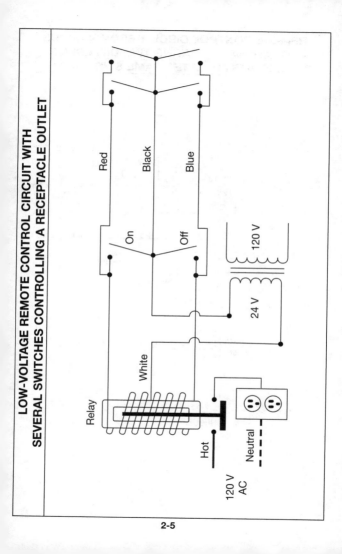

LOW-VOLTAGE REMOTE CONTROL CIRCUIT WITH
SEVERAL SWITCHES CONTROLLING A RECEPTACLE OUTLET

Red

Black

Blue

On

Off

120 V

24 V

White

Relay

Hot

Neutral

120 V
AC

2-5

REMOTE CONTROL CIRCUIT FROM VARIOUS LOCATIONS OPERATING TWO DIFFERENT CIRCUITS FROM THE SAME SWITCHES

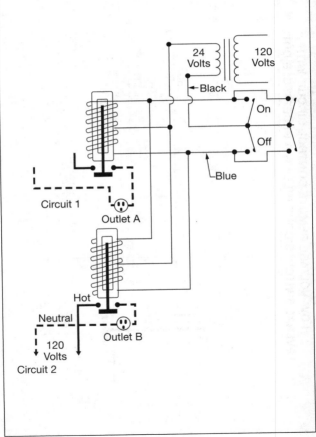

REMOTE CONTROL CIRCUIT CONTROLLING
THREE SEPARATE CIRCUITS WITH OUTLETS

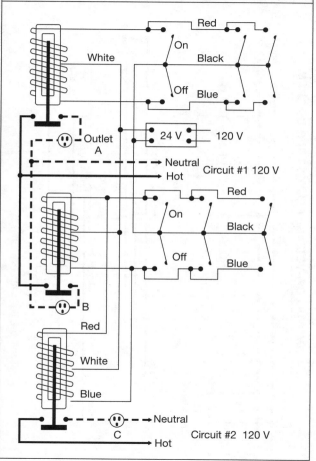

2-7

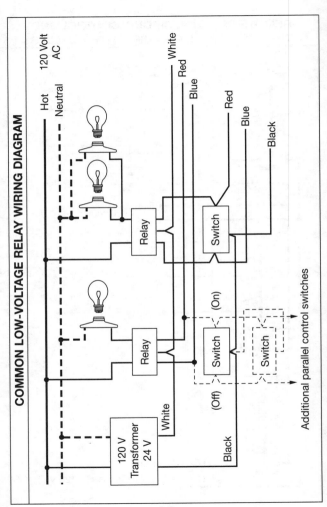

COMMON LOW-VOLTAGE RELAY WIRING DIAGRAM

120 Volt AC

Hot

Neutral

White
Red
Blue

Red

Blue

Black

Relay

Relay

Switch

Switch

Switch (On)

Switch (Off)

120 V Transformer 24 V

White

Black

Additional parallel control switches

2-8

WIRING DIAGRAM FOR A NINE POINT SELECTOR SWITCH

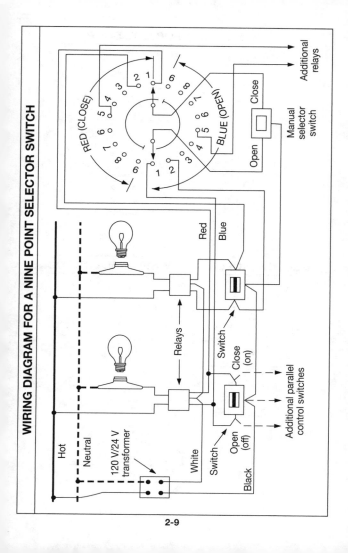

BELL CIRCUIT FOR ONE DOOR

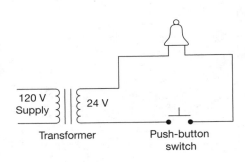

120 V
Supply

24 V

Transformer

Push-button
switch

BELL CONTROLLED FROM SEVERAL LOCATIONS

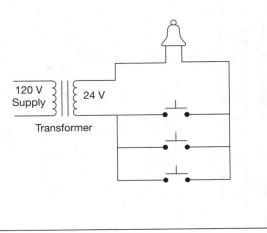

120 V
Supply

24 V

Transformer

RETURN CALL BELL SYSTEM

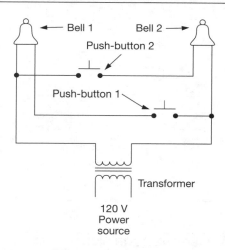

Bell 1 ← → Bell 2

Push-button 2

Push-button 1

Transformer

120 V
Power
source

RETURN CALL BELL SYSTEM UTILIZING
DOUBLE CONTACT PUSH-BUTTON SWITCHES

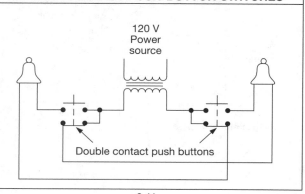

120 V
Power
source

Double contact push buttons

CENTRAL CHIME FOR TWO DOORS

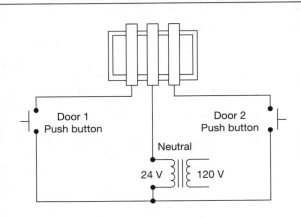

Door 1
Push button

Door 2
Push button

Neutral

24 V   120 V

THREE TONE DOOR SIGNAL SYSTEMS

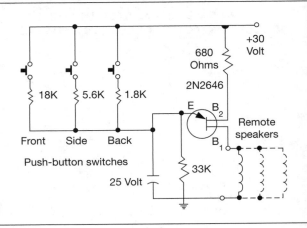

+30 Volt

680 Ohms

2N2646

18K   5.6K   1.8K

E   B₂

Remote speakers

B₁

Front   Side   Back

Push-button switches

33K

25 Volt

TWO PARALLEL-WIRED CHIMES

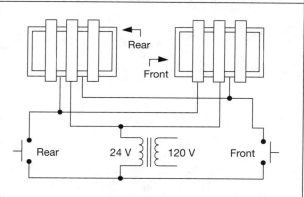

CHIME SYSTEM WITH
HOUSE NUMBER LIGHT AND TRANSFORMER

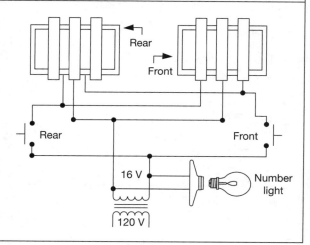

CLOSED CIRCUIT INTRUDER ALARM

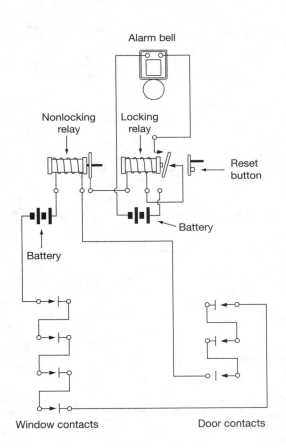

Alarm bell

Nonlocking relay

Locking relay

Reset button

Battery

Battery

Window contacts

Door contacts

OPEN CIRCUIT INTRUDER ALARM

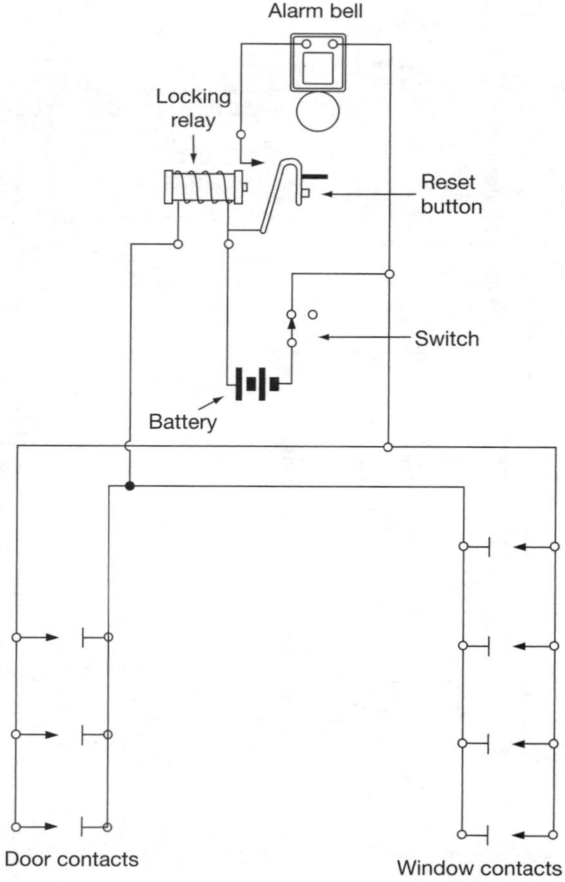

Alarm bell

Locking relay

Reset button

Switch

Battery

Door contacts

Window contacts

2-15

INTRUDER ALARM CIRCUIT WITH ANNUNCIATOR AND RELAY

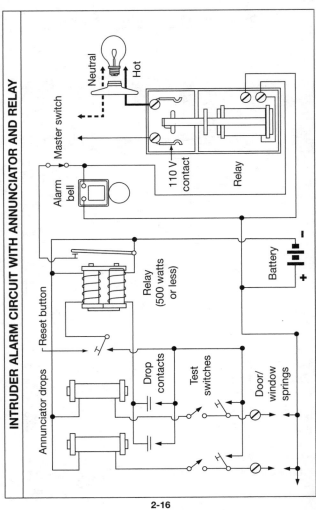

UNBALANCED AUDIO OUTPUT

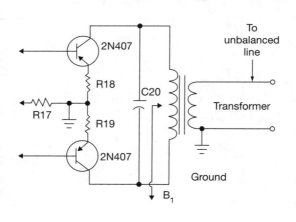

BALANCED AUDIO OUTPUT

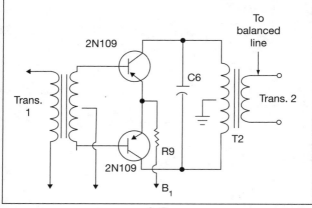

2-17

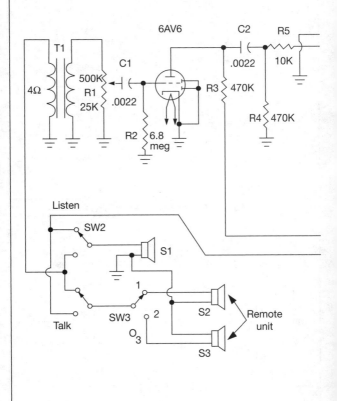

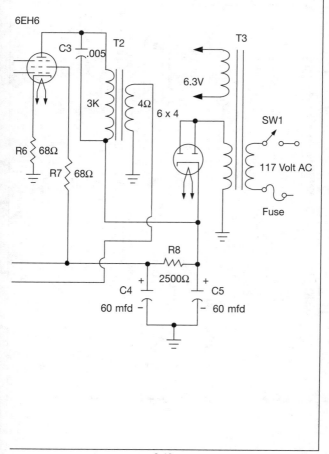

BASIC ANNUNCIATOR WIRING DIAGRAM

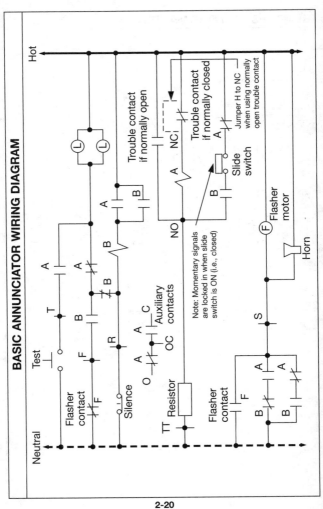

SEQUENCE SYSTEM FOR THERMAL POWER RELAYS

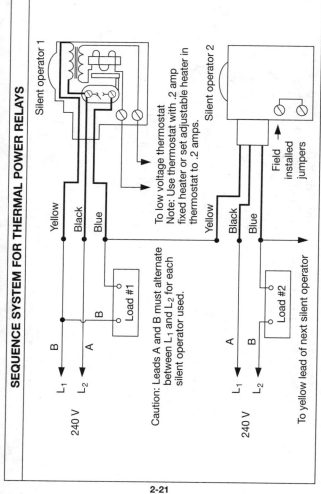

Silent operator 1

Silent operator 2

Yellow

Black

Blue

To low voltage thermostat
Note: Use thermostat with .2 amp
fixed heater or set adjustable heater in
thermostat to .2 amps.

Yellow

Black

Blue

Field
installed
jumpers

Load #1

Caution: Leads A and B must alternate
between L₁ and L₂ for each
silent operator used.

Load #2

L₁

240 V

L₂

B

A

B

L₁

240 V

L₂

A

B

To yellow lead of next silent operator

2-21

RESIDENTIAL POWERLINE CARRIER SYSTEM USING
NORMAL ELECTRIC CIRCUITS AS COMMUNICATION LINES

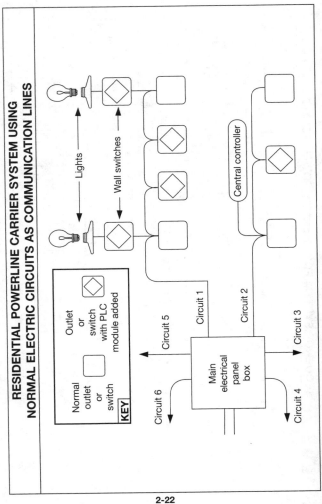

Lights

Wall switches

Central controller

Circuit 1

Circuit 2

Circuit 3

Circuit 4

Circuit 5

Circuit 6

Main electrical panel box

KEY

Normal outlet or switch

Outlet or switch with PLC module added

RESIDENTIAL HARD-WIRED CONTROL SYSTEM

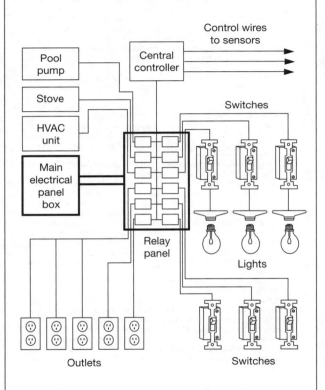

Control wires to sensors

Central controller

Pool pump

Stove

HVAC unit

Main electrical panel box

Switches

Relay panel

Lights

Outlets

Switches

From main panel, power goes to relay panel. Separate relays operate various equipment and are controlled via central controller.

COMMON TELEPHONE CONNECTIONS

The most common and simplest type of communication installation is the single line telephone. The typical telephone cable (sometimes called quad cable) contains four wires, colored green, red, black, and yellow. A one line telephone requires only two wires to operate. In almost all circumstances, green and red are the two conductors used. In a common four-wire modular connector, the green and red conductors are found in the inside positions, with the black and yellow wires in the outer positions.

As long as the two center conductors of the jack (again, always green and red) are connected to live phone lines, the telephone should operate.

Two-line phones generally use the same four wire cables and jacks. In this case, however, the inside two wires (green and red) carry line 1, and the outside two wires (black and yellow) carry line 2.

COLOR CODING OF CABLES

The color coding of twisted-pair cable uses a color pattern that identifies not only what conductors make up a pair but also what pair in the sequence it is, relative to other pairs within a multipair sheath. This is also used to determine which conductor in a pair is the *tip* conductor and which is the *ring* conductor. (The tip conductor is the positive conductor, and the ring conductor is the negative conductor.)

The banding scheme uses two opposing colors to represent a single pair. One color is considered the primary while the other color is considered the secondary. For example, given the primary color of white and the secondary color of blue, a single twisted-pair would consist of one cable that is white with blue bands on it. The five primary colors are white, red, black, yellow, and violet.

In multi-pair cables the primary color is responsible for an entire group of pairs (five pairs total). For example, the first five pairs all have the primary color of white. Each of the secondary colors, blue, orange, green, brown, and slate, are paired in a banded fashion with white. This continues through the entire primary color scheme for all four primary colors (comprising 25 individual pairs). In larger cables (50 pairs and up), each 25-pair group is wrapped in a pair of ribbons, again representing the groups of primary colors matched with their respective secondary colors. These color coded band markings help cable technicians to quickly identify and properly terminate cable pairs.

EIA COLOR CODE

You should note that the new EIA color code calls for the following color coding:

Pair 1	–	White/Blue (white with blue stripe) and Blue
Pair 2	–	White/Orange and Orange
Pair 3	–	White/Green and Green
Pair 4	–	White/Brown and Brown

STANDARD TELECOM COLOR CODING

PAIR #	TIP (+) COLOR	RING (–) COLOR
1	White	Blue
2	White	Orange
3	White	Green
4	White	Brown
5	White	Slate
6	Red	Blue
7	Red	Orange
8	Red	Green
9	Red	Brown
10	Red	Slate
11	Black	Blue
12	Black	Orange
13	Black	Green
14	Black	Brown
15	Black	Slate
16	Yellow	Blue
17	Yellow	Orange
18	Yellow	Green
19	Yellow	Brown
20	Yellow	Slate
21	Violet	Blue
22	Violet	Orange
23	Violet	Green
24	Violet	Brown
25	Violet	Slate

MODULAR JACK STYLES

8-Position

8-Position Keyed

6-Position

6-Position Modified

There are four basic modular jack styles. The 8-position and 8-position keyed modular jacks are commonly and incorrectly referred to as RJ45 and keyed RJ45 (respectively). The 6-position modular jack is commonly referred to as RJ11. Using these terms can sometimes lead to confusion since the RJ designations actually refer to very specific wiring configurations called Universal Service Ordering Codes (USOC). The designation 'RJ' means Registered Jack. Each of these 3 basic jack styles can be wired for different RJ configurations. For example, the 6-position jack can be wired as a RJ11C (1-Pair), RJ14C (2-Pair), or RJ25C (3-Pair) configuration. An 8-position jack can be wired for configurations such as RJ61C (4-Pair) and RJ48C. The keyed 8-position jack can be wired for RJ45S, RJ46S and RJ47S. The fourth modular jack style is a modified version of the 6-position jack (modified modular jack or MMJ). It was designed by DEC along with the modified modular plug (MMP) to eliminate the possibility of connecting DEC data equipment to voice lines and vice versa.

COMMON WIRING CONFIGURATIONS

The TIA and AT&T wiring schemes are the two that have been adopted by EIA/TIA-568. They are nearly identical except that pairs two and three are reversed. TIA is the preferred scheme because it is compatible with 1 or 2-pair USOC Systems. Either configuration can be used for Integrated Services Digital Network (ISDN) applications.

Pair ID	PIN #
T1	5
R1	4
T2	3
R2	6
T3	1
R3	2
T4	7
R4	8

TIA (T568A)

Pair ID	PIN #
T1	5
R1	4
T2	1
R2	2
T3	3
R3	6
T4	7
R4	8

AT&T (T568B)

USOC wiring is available for 1-, 2-, 3-, or 4-pair systems. Pair 1 occupies the center conductors, pair 2 occupies the next two contacts out, etc. One advantage to this scheme is that a 6-position plug configured with 1, 2, or 3 pairs can be inserted into an 8-position jack and maintain pair continuity; a note of warning though, pins 1 and 8 on the jack may become damaged from this practice. A disadvantage is the poor transmission performance associated with this type of pair sequence.

Pair ID	PIN #
T1	5
R1	4
T2	3
R2	6
T3	2
R3	7
T4	1
R4	8

USOC 4-Pair

Pair ID	PIN #
T1	4
R1	3
T2	2
R2	5
T3	1
R3	6

USOC 1-, 2-, or 3-Pair

ETHERNET 10BASE-T

Ethernet 10BASE-T wiring specifies an 8-position jack but uses only two pairs. These are pairs two and three of TIA schemes.

Pair ID	PIN #
T1	1
R1	2
T2	3
R2	6

25-PAIR COLOR CODING/ISDN CONTACT ASSIGNMENTS

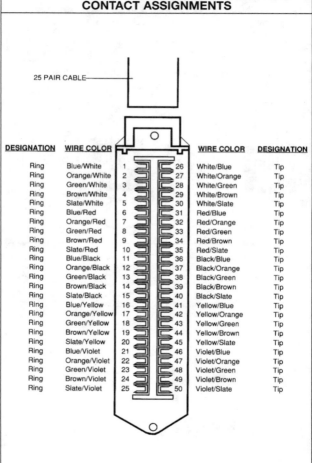

25 PAIR CABLE

DESIGNATION	WIRE COLOR			WIRE COLOR	DESIGNATION
Ring	Blue/White	1	26	White/Blue	Tip
Ring	Orange/White	2	27	White/Orange	Tip
Ring	Green/White	3	28	White/Green	Tip
Ring	Brown/White	4	29	White/Brown	Tip
Ring	Slate/White	5	30	White/Slate	Tip
Ring	Blue/Red	6	31	Red/Blue	Tip
Ring	Orange/Red	7	32	Red/Orange	Tip
Ring	Green/Red	8	33	Red/Green	Tip
Ring	Brown/Red	9	34	Red/Brown	Tip
Ring	Slate/Red	10	35	Red/Slate	Tip
Ring	Blue/Black	11	36	Black/Blue	Tip
Ring	Orange/Black	12	37	Black/Orange	Tip
Ring	Green/Black	13	38	Black/Green	Tip
Ring	Brown/Black	14	39	Black/Brown	Tip
Ring	Slate/Black	15	40	Black/Slate	Tip
Ring	Blue/Yellow	16	41	Yellow/Blue	Tip
Ring	Orange/Yellow	17	42	Yellow/Orange	Tip
Ring	Green/Yellow	18	43	Yellow/Green	Tip
Ring	Brown/Yellow	19	44	Yellow/Brown	Tip
Ring	Slate/Yellow	20	45	Yellow/Slate	Tip
Ring	Blue/Violet	21	46	Violet/Blue	Tip
Ring	Orange/Violet	22	47	Violet/Orange	Tip
Ring	Green/Violet	23	48	Violet/Green	Tip
Ring	Brown/Violet	24	49	Violet/Brown	Tip
Ring	Slate/Violet	25	50	Violet/Slate	Tip

COMMON UNSHIELDED TWISTED PAIR
DATA AND VOICE WIRING SCHEMES

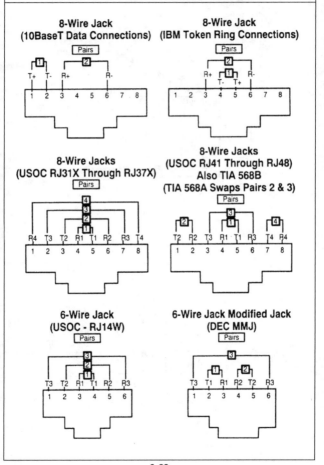

8-Wire Jack
(10BaseT Data Connections)

8-Wire Jack
(IBM Token Ring Connections)

8-Wire Jacks
(USOC RJ31X Through RJ37X)

8-Wire Jacks
(USOC RJ41 Through RJ48)
Also TIA 568B
(TIA 568A Swaps Pairs 2 & 3)

6-Wire Jack
(USOC - RJ14W)

6-Wire Jack Modified Jack
(DEC MMJ)

DATA AND VOICE WIRING DIAGRAMS

RJ31X

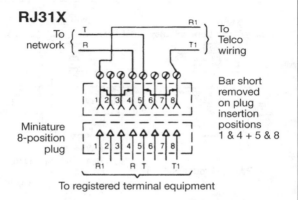

To network { T R }

R1

To Telco wiring

T1

Miniature 8-position plug

Bar short removed on plug insertion positions 1 & 4 + 5 & 8

1 2 3 4 5 6 7 8

R1   R   T   T1

To registered terminal equipment

RJ32X

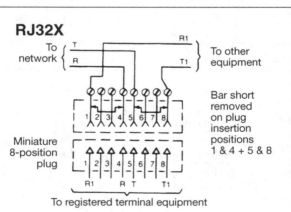

To network { T R }

R1

To other equipment

T1

Miniature 8-position plug

Bar short removed on plug insertion positions 1 & 4 + 5 & 8

1 2 3 4 5 6 7 8

R1   R   T   T1

To registered terminal equipment

DATA AND VOICE WIRING DIAGRAMS *(cont.)*

RJ33X

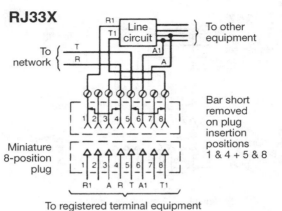

To other equipment

To network

Bar short removed on plug insertion positions 1 & 4 + 5 & 8

Miniature 8-position plug

To registered terminal equipment

RJ34X

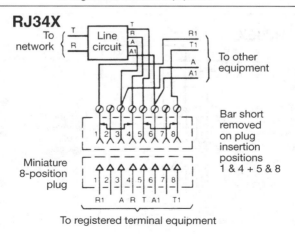

To network

To other equipment

Bar short removed on plug insertion positions 1 & 4 + 5 & 8

Miniature 8-position plug

To registered terminal equipment

RJ35X

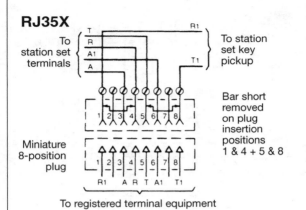

To station set terminals: T, R, A1, A

To station set key pickup: R1, T1

Bar short removed on plug insertion positions 1 & 4 + 5 & 8

Miniature 8-position plug

1 2 3 4 5 6 7 8
R1 A R T A1 T1

To registered terminal equipment

RJ36X

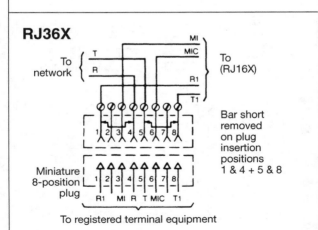

To network: T, R

To (RJ16X): MI, MIC, R1, T1

Bar short removed on plug insertion positions 1 & 4 + 5 & 8

Miniature 8-position plug

1 2 3 4 5 6 7 8
R1 MI R T MIC T1

To registered terminal equipment

RJ37X

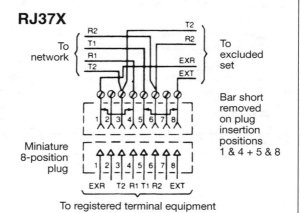

To network { R2 T1 R1 T2

T2 R2 EXR EXT } To excluded set

Bar short removed on plug insertion positions 1 & 4 + 5 & 8

Miniature 8-position plug

1 2 3 4 5 6 7 8
EXR T2 R1 T1 R2 EXT

To registered terminal equipment

RJ38X

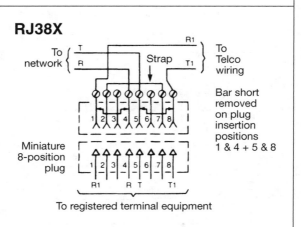

To network { T R

R1 T1 } To Telco wiring

Strap

Bar short removed on plug insertion positions 1 & 4 + 5 & 8

Miniature 8-position plug

1 2 3 4 5 6 7 8
R1 R T T1

To registered terminal equipment

DATA AND VOICE WIRING DIAGRAMS *(cont.)*

Electrical Network Connection
Single line bridged tip and ring with programming resistor.

Mechanical Arrangement
Miniature eight-position keyed jack.

Typical Usage
Connects computers and other data equipment to the telephone network.

RJ41S

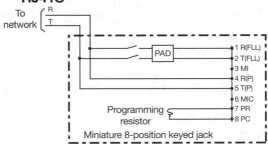

RJ45S

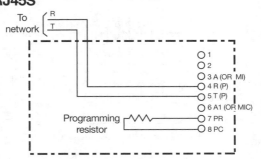

Electrical Network Connection
Up to four line T/R.

Mechanical Arrangement
Miniature eight-position modular jack.

Typical Usage
Connects up to four lines to a single telephone set or other device. Commonly used for telephones requiring separate power pairs and/or separate signaling pairs.

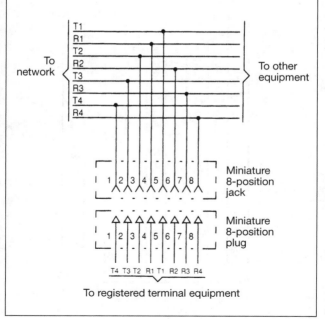

To network

To other equipment

T1
R1
T2
R2
T3
R3
T4
R4

Miniature 8-position jack

1 2 3 4 5 6 7 8

Miniature 8-position plug

1 2 3 4 5 6 7 8

T4 T3 T2 R1 T1 R2 R3 R4

To registered terminal equipment

ISDN ASSIGNMENT OF CONTACT NUMBERS

Table contact assignments for plugs and jacks:

Contact Number	TE	NT	Polarity
1	Power source 3	Power sink 3	+
2	Power source 3	Power sink 3	−
3	Transmit	Receive	+
4	Receive	Transmit	+
5	Receive	Transmit	−
6	Transmit	Receive	−
7	Power sink 2	Power source 2	−
8	Power sink 2	Power source 2	+

8P8C (ISDN)

TYPICAL WIRING METHODS

Loop Series Wiring

Parallel Distribution Wiring

2-Line System

Electronic Key Systems

SIDE #2

	White/Blue
	Blue/White
	White/Orange
	Orange/White
	White/Green
	Green/White
	White/Brown
	Brown/White
	White/Slate
	Slate/White
	Red/Blue
	Blue/Red
	Red/Orange
	Orange/Red
	Red/Green
	Green/Red
	Red/Brown
	Brown/Red
	Red/Slate
	Slate/Red
	Black/Blue
	Blue/Black
	Black/Orange
	Orange/Black
	Black/Green
	Green/Black

TOP

PAIR CODE		SIDE #1	
Pair 1	Tip 26	White/Blue	
	Ring 1	Blue/White	
Pair 2	Tip 27	White/Orange	
	Ring 2	Orange/White	
Pair 3	Tip 28	White/Green	
	Ring 3	Green/White	
Pair 4	Tip 29	White/Brown	
	Ring 4	Brown/White	
Pair 5	Tip 30	White/Slate	
	Ring 5	Slate/White	
Pair 6	Tip 31	Red/Blue	
	Ring 6	Blue/Red	
Pair 7	Tip 32	Red/Orange	
	Ring 7	Orange/Red	
Pair 8	Tip 33	Red/Green	
	Ring 8	Green/Red	
Pair 9	Tip 34	Red/Brown	
	Ring 9	Brown/Red	
Pair 10	Tip 35	Red/Slate	
	Ring 10	Slate/Red	
Pair 11	Tip 36	Black/Blue	
	Ring 11	Blue/Black	
Pair 12	Tip 37	Black/Orange	
	Ring 12	Orange/Black	
Pair 13	Tip 38	Black/Green	
	Ring 13	Green/Black	

CABLE COLOR CODING

		Top labels
		Black/Brown
		Brown/Black
		Black/Slate
		Slate/Black
		Yellow/Blue
		Blue/Yellow
		Yellow/Orange
		Orange/Yellow
		Yellow/Green
		Green/Yellow
		Yellow/Brown
		Brown/Yellow
		Yellow/Slate
		Slate/Yellow
		Violet/Blue
		Blue/Violet
		Violet/Orange
		Orange/Violet
		Violet/Green
		Green/Violet
		Violet/Brown
		Brown/Violet
		Violet/Slate
		Slate/Violet

Pair	Tip/Ring	Color
Pair 14	Tip 39	Black/Brown
	Ring 14	Brown/Black
Pair 15	Tip 40	Black/Slate
	Ring 15	Slate/Black
Pair 16	Tip 41	Yellow/Blue
	Ring 16	Blue/Yellow
Pair 17	Tip 42	Yellow/Orange
	Ring 17	Orange/Yellow
Pair 18	Tip 43	Yellow/Green
	Ring 18	Green/Yellow
Pair 19	Tip 44	Yellow/Brown
	Ring 19	Brown/Yellow
Pair 20	Tip 45	Yellow/Slate
	Ring 20	Slate/Yellow
Pair 21	Tip 46	Violet/Blue
	Ring 21	Blue/Violet
Pair 22	Tip 47	Violet/Orange
	Ring 22	Orange/Violet
Pair 23	Tip 48	Violet/Green
	Ring 23	Green/Violet
Pair 24	Tip 49	Violet/Brown
	Ring 24	Brown/Violet
Pair 25	Tip 50	Violet/Slate
	Ring 25	Slate/Violet

150-PAIR PIC CABLE
CORE ARRANGEMENT

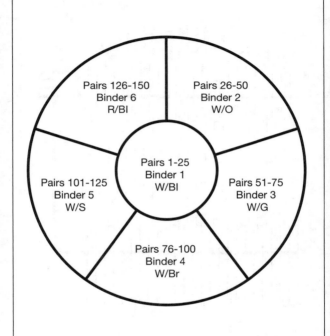

Pairs 126-150
Binder 6
R/Bl

Pairs 26-50
Binder 2
W/O

Pairs 1-25
Binder 1
W/Bl

Pairs 101-125
Binder 5
W/S

Pairs 51-75
Binder 3
W/G

Pairs 76-100
Binder 4
W/Br

PHANTOM TELEPHONE CIRCUIT

Side Circuit 1

Phantom Circuit

Side Circuit 2

Cable or wire pair

STANDARD DTMF PAD AND FREQUENCIES

(Low Group)

697Hz >

770Hz >

825Hz >

941Hz >

1	2	3	A
4	5	6	B
7	8	9	C
*	0	#	D

^1209Hz ^1336Hz ^1477Hz ^1633Hz

(High Group)

WIREMAPPING

Wiremap tests will check all lines in the cable for all of the following errors:

- **Open:** Lack of continuity between pins at both ends of the cable.

- **Short:** Two or more lines short-circuited together.

- **Crossed pair:** A pair is connected to different pins at each end (example: pair 1 is connected to pins 4 & 5 at one end, and pins 1 & 2 at the other).

- **Reversed pair:** The two lines in a pair are connected to opposite pins at each end of the cable. For example: the line on pin 1 is connected to pin 2 at the other end, the line on pin 2 is connected to line 1. This is also called a *polarity reversal or tip-and-ring reversal.*

- **Split pair:** One line from each of two pairs is connected as if it were a pair. For example, the Blue and White-Orange lines are connected to pins 4 & 5, White-Blue and Orange pins to 3 & 6. The result is excessive Near End Crosstalk (NEXT), which wastes 10Base-T bandwidth and usually prevents 16 Mb/s token-ring from working at all.

EIA/TIA 568A
MODULAR PIN CONNECTIONS

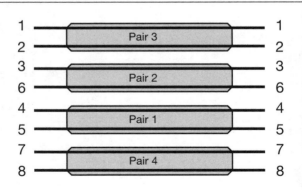

MODULAR PIN CONNECTIONS — REVERSED PAIR

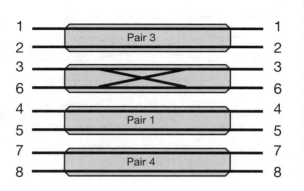

MODULAR PIN CONNECTIONS — SHORTS AND OPENS

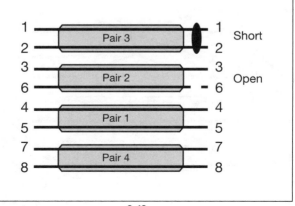

MODULAR PIN CONNECTIONS — SPLIT PAIRS

```
1 ─────                       ───── 1
2 ─────        ╲   ╱          ───── 2
3 ─────         ╳             ───── 3
6 ─────        ╱   ╲          ───── 6

4 ─────┌─────────────────────┐───── 4
5 ─────│        Pair 1        │───── 5

7 ─────┌─────────────────────┐───── 7
8 ─────│        Pair 4        │───── 8
```

**MODULAR PIN CONNECTIONS —
TRANSPOSED OR CROSSED PAIRS**

```
1 ─────      ╲       ╱        ───── 1
2 ─────       ╲     ╱         ───── 2
3 ─────        ╳   ╳          ───── 3
6 ─────       ╱     ╲         ───── 6

4 ─────┌─────────────────────┐───── 4
5 ─────│        Pair 1        │───── 5

7 ─────┌─────────────────────┐───── 7
8 ─────│        Pair 4        │───── 8
```

BALANCED PAIR TRANSMISSION

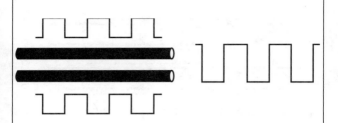

Equal but opposite signals on a pair of wires.

Output is sum of both signals.

ATTENUATION

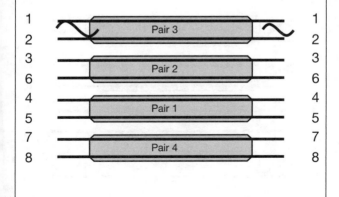

NEXT (NEAR END CROSSTALK)

1	Pair 3	1
2		2
3	Pair 2	3
6		6
4	Pair 1	4
5		5
7	Pair 4	7
8		8

POWER SUM NEXT (NEAR END CROSSTALK)

1	Pair 3	1
2		2
3	Pair 2	3
6		6
4	Pair 1	4
5		5
7	Pair 4	7
8		8

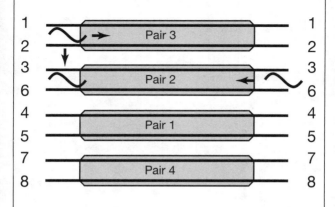

ACR (ATTENUATION TO CROSSTALK RATIO)

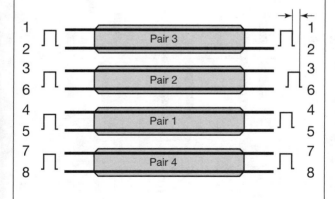

DELAY SKEW

NEURON CHIP SIMPLIFIED BLOCK DIAGRAM

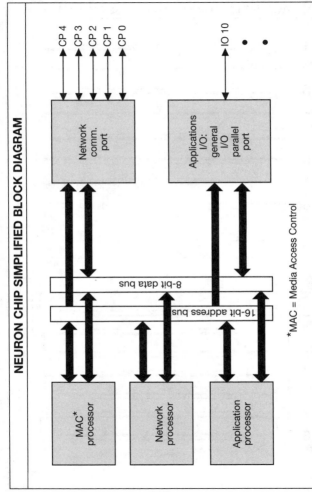

CP 4
CP 3
CP 2
CP 1
CP 0

IO 10 • •

Network comm. port

Applications I/O: general I/O parallel port

8-bit data bus

16-bit address bus

MAC* processor

Network processor

Application processor

*MAC = Media Access Control

2-48

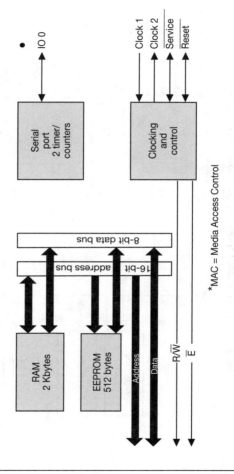

*MAC = Media Access Control

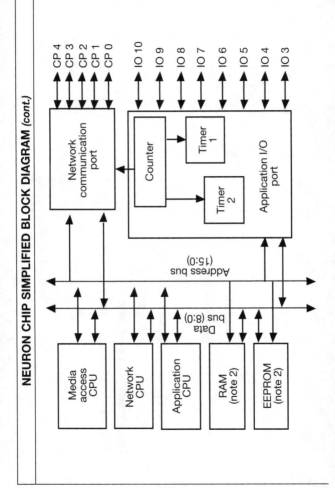

NEURON CHIP SIMPLIFIED BLOCK DIAGRAM *(cont.)*

CP 4
CP 3
CP 2
CP 1
CP 0

IO 10
IO 9
IO 8
IO 7
IO 6
IO 5
IO 4
IO 3

Network communication port

Counter

Timer 1

Timer 2

Application I/O port

Address bus (15:0)

Data bus (8:0)

Media access CPU

Network CPU

Application CPU

RAM (note 2)

EEPROM (note 2)

2-50

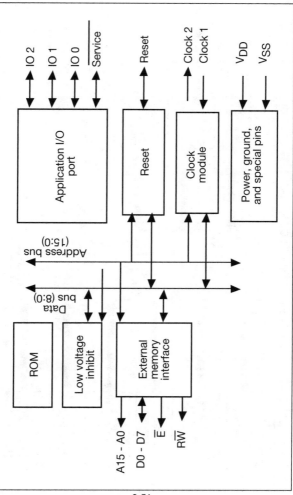

IO 2
IO 1
IO 0
Service

Reset

Clock 2
Clock 1

V_DD
V_SS

Application I/O port

Reset

Clock module

Power, ground, and special pins

Address bus (15:0)

Data bus (8:0)

ROM

Low voltage inhibit

External memory interface

A15 - A0
D0 - D7
E
RW

2-51

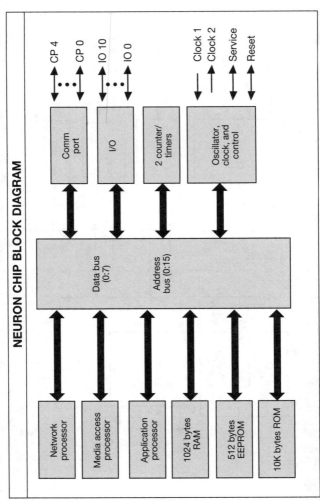

NEURON CHIP BLOCK DIAGRAM

CP 4
CP 0
IO 10
IO 0
Clock 1
Clock 2
Service
Reset

Comm port
I/O
2 counter/timers
Oscillator, clock, and control

Data bus (0:7)
Address bus (0:15)

Network processor
Media access processor
Application processor
1024 bytes RAM
512 bytes EEPROM
10K bytes ROM

2-52

BASIC HVAC THERMOSTAT CIRCUIT

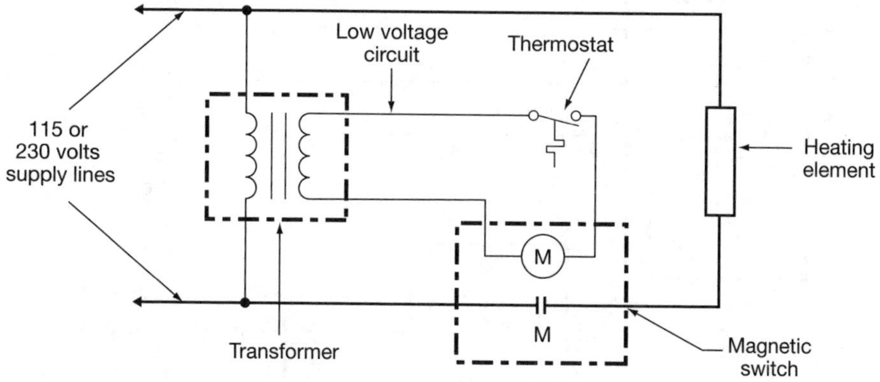

Heating element

Magnetic switch

Thermostat

M

M

Low voltage circuit

Transformer

115 or 230 volts supply lines

2-53

HVAC TWIN-TYPE THERMOSTAT

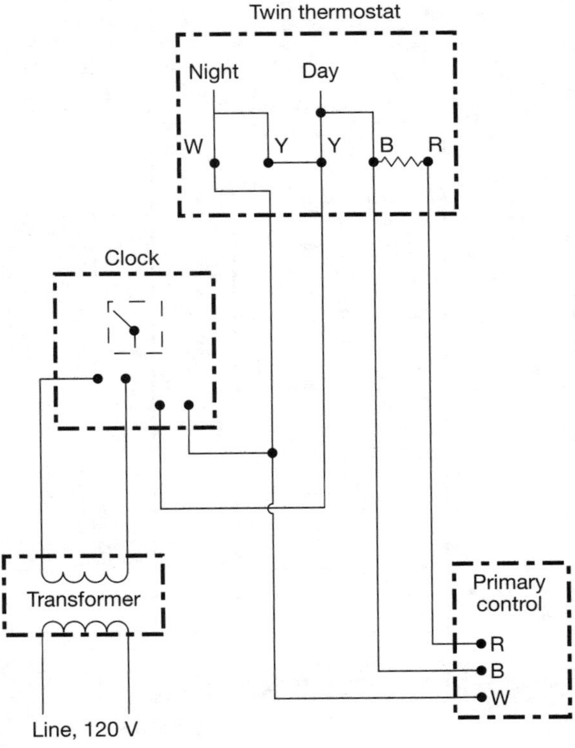

Twin thermostat

Night   Day

W   Y   Y   B   R

Clock

Transformer

Line, 120 V

Primary control

R
B
W

HVAC MILLIVOLT CONTROL

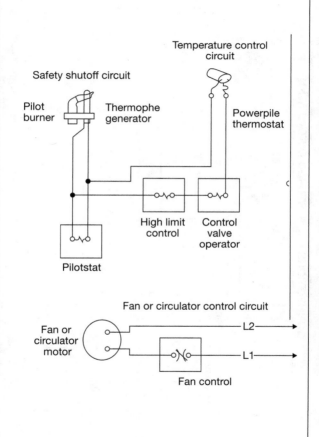

Temperature control circuit

Safety shutoff circuit

Pilot burner

Thermophe generator

Powerpile thermostat

High limit control

Control valve operator

Pilotstat

Fan or circulator control circuit

Fan or circulator motor

L2

L1

Fan control

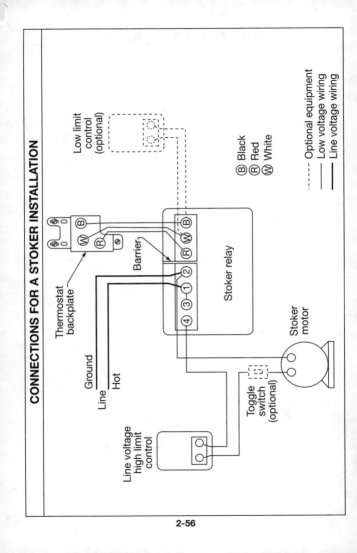

CONNECTIONS FOR A STOKER INSTALLATION

Low limit control (optional)

Thermostat backplate

Barrier

Stoker relay

Stoker motor

Ground

Line

Hot

Line voltage high limit control

Toggle switch (optional)

Ⓑ Black
Ⓡ Red
Ⓦ White

---- Optional equipment
—— Low voltage wiring
—— Line voltage wiring

2-56

CONNECTIONS FOR AN OIL BURNER INSTALLATION

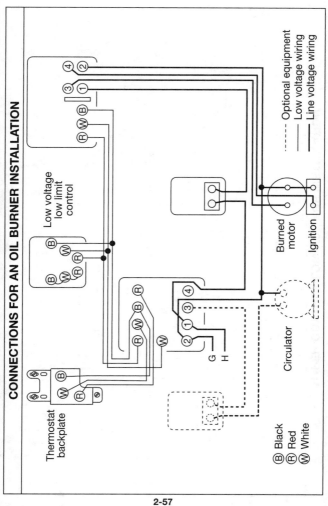

Low voltage low limit control

Thermostat backplate

Burned motor

Ignition

Circulator

---- Optional equipment
—— Low voltage wiring
━━ Line voltage wiring

B Black
R Red
W White

DAMPER-CONTROL LOW-VOLTAGE INSTALLATION

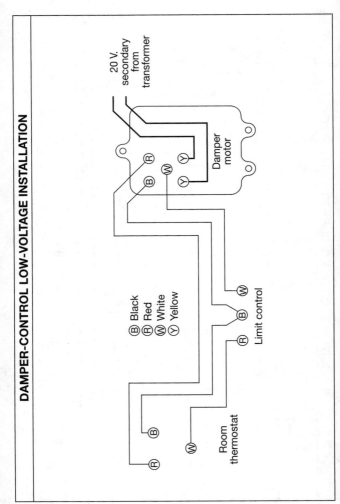

20 V. secondary from transformer

Damper motor

Ⓑ Black
Ⓡ Red
Ⓦ White
Ⓨ Yellow

Limit control

Room thermostat

2-58

GAS BURNER CONTROLS

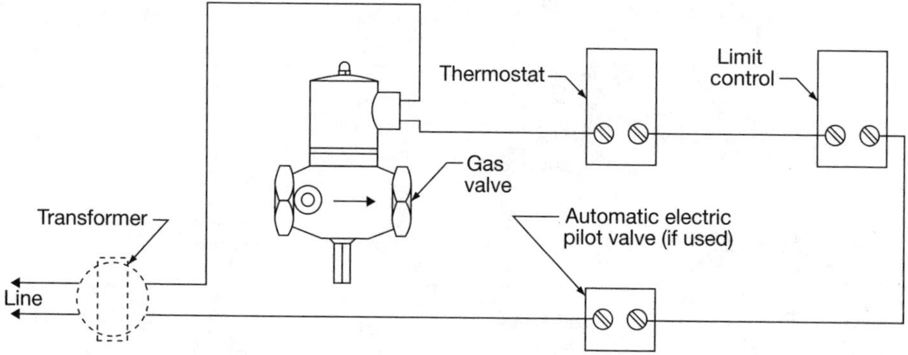

Limit control

Automatic electric pilot valve (if used)

Thermostat

Gas valve

Transformer

Line

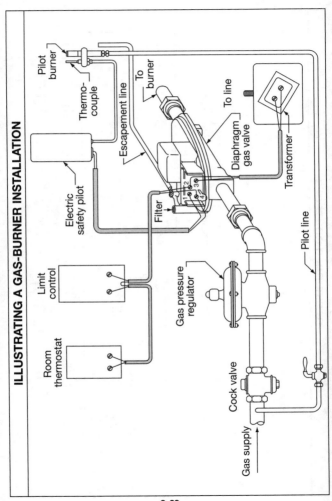

ILLUSTRATING A GAS-BURNER INSTALLATION

Pilot burner

Thermo-couple

Escapement line

To burner

To line

Diaphragm gas valve

Transformer

Electric safety pilot

Filter

Limit control

Room thermostat

Gas pressure regulator

Pilot line

Cock valve

Gas supply

2-60

ELECTRIC HEATING UNIT DIAGRAMS

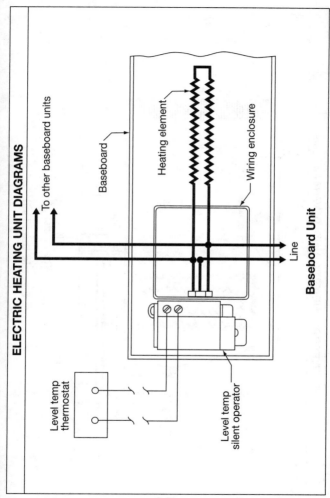

To other baseboard units

Baseboard

Heating element

Wiring enclosure

Line

Level temp thermostat

Level temp silent operator

Baseboard Unit

2-61

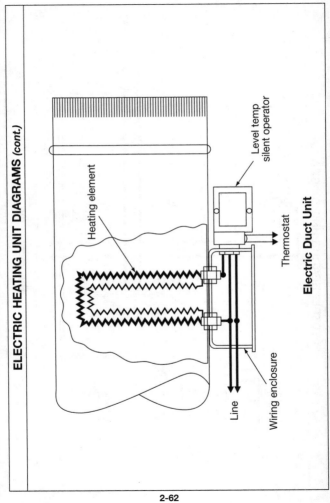

Heating element

Level temp silent operator

Thermostat

Line

Wiring enclosure

Electric Duct Unit

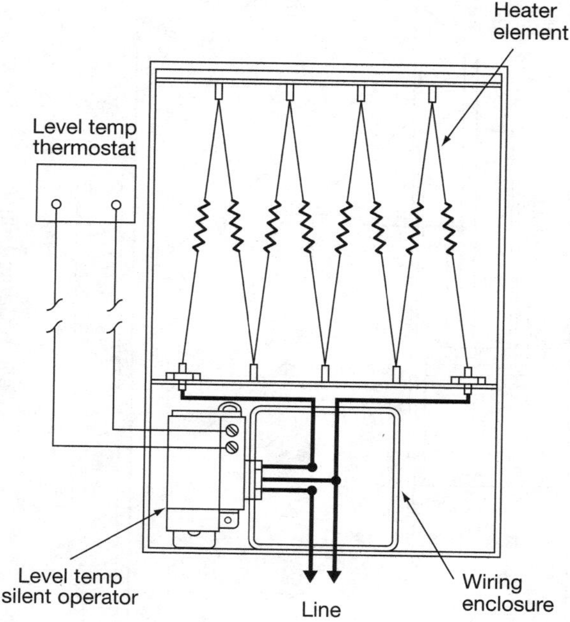

Heater element

Level temp thermostat

Level temp silent operator

Line

Wiring enclosure

Wall or Ceiling Unit

ELECTRIC HEATING UNIT DIAGRAMS (cont.)

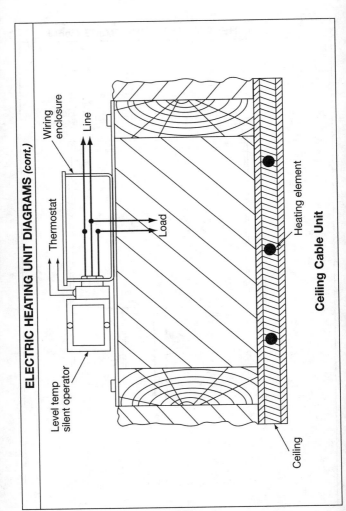

Ceiling Cable Unit

Line

Wiring enclosure

Thermostat

Load

Level temp silent operator

Heating element

Ceiling

COMPOUND METAL THERMOSTAT AND CIRCUIT

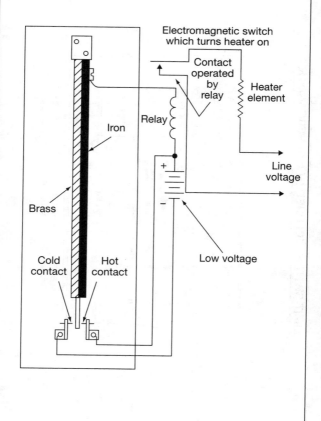

Electromagnetic switch
which turns heater on

Contact
operated
by relay

Heater
element

Relay

Iron

Brass

Line
voltage

Low voltage

Cold
contact

Hot
contact

LIMIT SWITCH INCLUDED IN A BASEBOARD HEATER

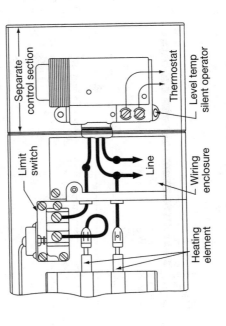

CHAPTER 3
Grounding

Grounding is critical for safety. Essentially, there are two purposes for grounding:

1. **To provide a reliable return path for errant currents.**
2. **To provide protection from lightning.**

At first, it might seem better not to provide a good return path for errant currents, thus making it harder for them to flow. While this method would certainly be effective in reducing the size of *fault currents* (currents that flow where they are not intended), it would also allow them to flow more or less continually when they occur.

Since it is these fault currents that pose the greatest danger to people, our primary concern is to eliminate them entirely. We do this by providing a clear path (one with virtually zero resistance — a "dead" short circuit) back to the power source, so that these currents will be very large and thus activate the fuse or circuit breaker. The overcurrent protective device will then cut off all current to the affected circuit, eliminating any danger. This also ensures that the circuit cannot be operated while the fault is present, which makes speedy repairs unavoidable.

To put things in simple terms, we could say that we use grounding to make sure that when circuits fail, they fail all the way. Partially failed circuits are the ones that are dangerous because they can go unnoticed; therefore, grounding is essential.

GROUNDING

The requirements for all types of grounding are covered in article 250 of the National Electrical Code (NEC). It is mandatory from both legal and safety standpoints that all systems be grounded according to these rules.

An electrical installation's *grounding electrode system* connects that system to ground. This is a critically important link in a grounding system, and requires carefully chosen materials and methods.

The *grounding electrode conductor* is the conductor that runs between the main service disconnect enclosure and a grounding electrode (most commonly a ground rod or cold-water pipe). This is a key element in completing the ground circuit, which, in turn, is necessary to ensure the safety of an electrical system.

The connection between a grounding electrode conductor and a grounding electrode must be accessible, permanent, and effective, since the safety of the entire system often depends on this connection.

All grounding connections must be listed means, and must be permanent and secure. If grounding connections are made in areas where they can be subjected to physical damage, they must be protected.

In general, the NEC requires a premise wiring system, supplied by an alternating-current service to be grounded by a grounding electrode conductor connected to a grounding electrode. The grounding electrode conductor must be bonded to the grounded service conductor (neutral) at any accessible point from the load end of the service drop or service lateral to, and including, the terminal bus to which the grounded service conductor is connected at the service disconnecting means. A grounding connection must not be made to any grounded circuit conductor on the load side of the service disconnecting means.

Most applications require the grounded service conductor to be bonded to at least two grounding electrodes according to NEC Section 250.81.

Effective Ground-Fault Current Path. An intentionally constructed, permanent, low-impedance electrically conductive path designed and intended to carry current under ground-fault conditions from the point of a ground fault on a wiring system to the electrical supply source.

Ground Fault. An unintentional, electrically conducting connection between an ungrounded conductor of an electrical circuit and the normally non-current-carrying conductors, metallic enclosures, metallic raceways, metallic equipment, or earth.

Ground-Fault Current Path. An electrically conductive path from the point of a ground fault on a wiring system through normally non-current-carrying conductors, equipment, or the earth to the electrical supply source. Ground-fault current paths could consist of any combination of equipment grounding conductors, metallic raceways, electrical equipment, metal water pipes, steel framing members, metal ducting, reinforcing steel and the earth itself.

BASIC GROUNDING CONNECTIONS

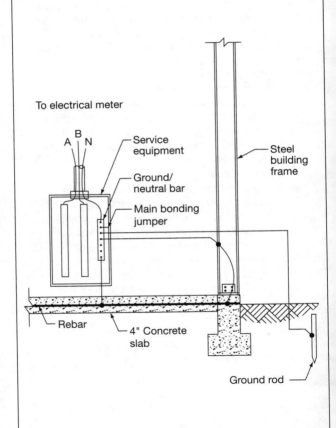

To electrical meter

A B N

Service equipment

Ground/neutral bar

Main bonding jumper

Steel building frame

Rebar

4" Concrete slab

Ground rod

MINIMUM SIZES OF GROUNDING ELECTRODE CONDUCTORS FOR AC SYSTEMS

Size of Largest Service-Entrance Conductor or Equivalent for Parallel Conductors		Size of Grounding Electrode Conductor	
Copper	Aluminum or Copper-Clad Aluminum	Copper	Aluminum or Copper-Clad Aluminum
2 or smaller	0 or smaller	8	6
1 or 2	2/0 or 3/0	6	4
2/0 or 3/0	4/0 or 250 kcmil	4	2
Over 3/0 through 350 kcmil	Over 250 kcmil through 500 kcmil	2	0
Over 350 kcmil through 600 kcmil	Over 500 kcmil through 900 kcmil	0	3/0
Over 600 kcmil through 1100 kcmil	Over 900 kcmil through 1750 kcmil	2/0	4/0
Over 1100 kcmil	Over 1750 kcmil	3/0	250 kcmil

RESISTIVITIES OF VARIOUS SOILS

TYPES OF SOIL	RESISTIVITY MEASURED IN OHMS PER CUBIC METER		
	Average	Min.	Max.
WASTE Fills—ashes, cinders, brine	2,370	590	7,000
Clay, shale, gumbo, loam	4,060	340	16,300
Same—with varying proportions of sand and gravel	15,800	1,020	135,000
Gravel, sand, stones, with little clay or loam	94,000	59,000	458,000

ADDING CHEMICALS TO SOIL TO LOWER GROUND RESISTANCE

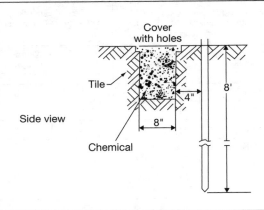

Side view

Cover with holes

Tile

Chemical

8'

4"

8"

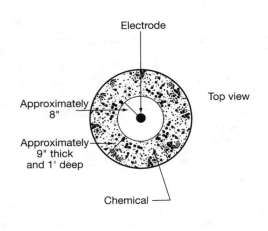

Top view

Electrode

Approximately 8"

Approximately 9" thick and 1' deep

Chemical

GROUND-ROD TESTING

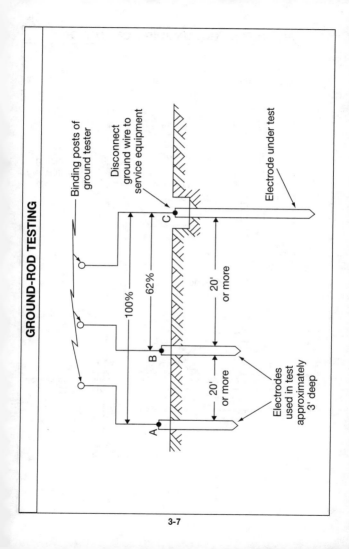

Binding posts of ground tester

Disconnect ground wire to service equipment

100%

62%

A

B

C

20'
or more

20'
or more

20'
or more

Electrodes used in test approximately 3' deep

Electrode under test

EQUIPMENT GROUNDING CONDUCTOR

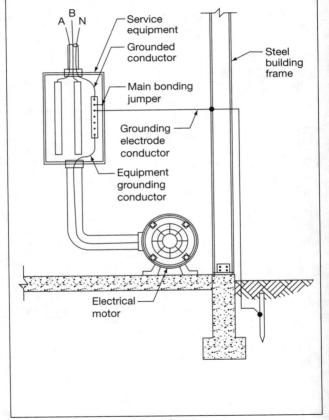

To electrical meter

A B N

Service equipment

Grounded conductor

Main bonding jumper

Grounding electrode conductor

Equipment grounding conductor

Steel building frame

Electrical motor

GROUNDED CONDUCTOR — NEUTRAL

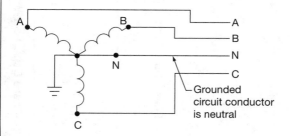

A
B
N
C
Grounded
circuit conductor
is neutral

3ϕ, 4-Wire Wye Grounded System

GROUNDED CONDUCTOR — NOT NEUTRAL

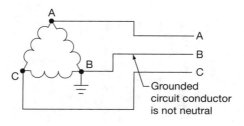

A
B
C
Grounded
circuit conductor
is not neutral

3ϕ, 3-Wire Corner-Grounded Delta System

GROUNDING DIFFERENT TYPES OF CIRCUITS

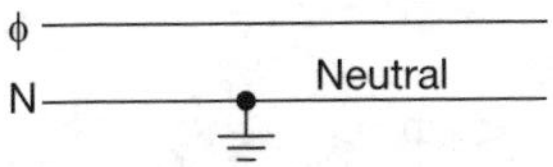

Single-Phase, Two-Wire

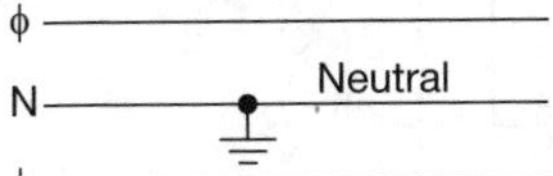

Single-Phase, Three-Wire

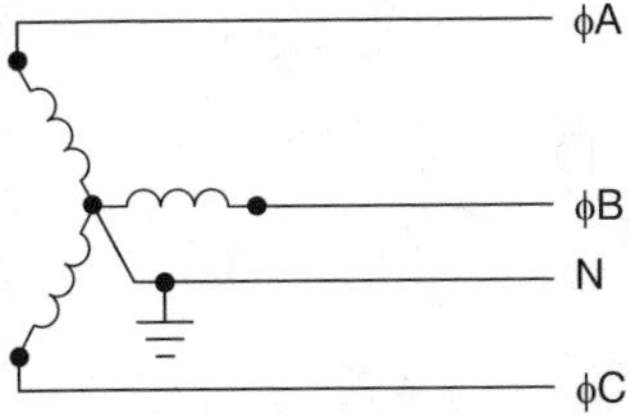

Three-Phase Wye

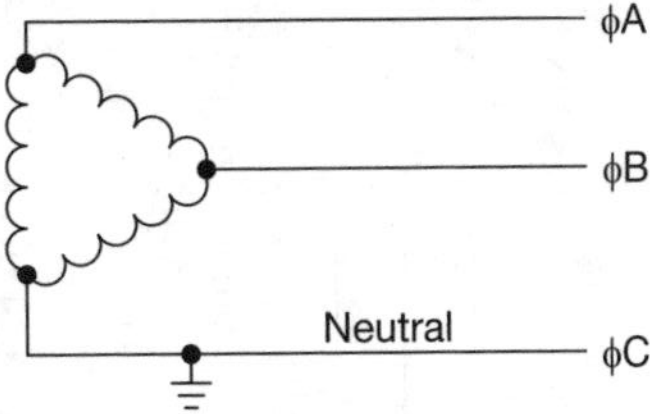

Three-Phase Delta, Three-Wire

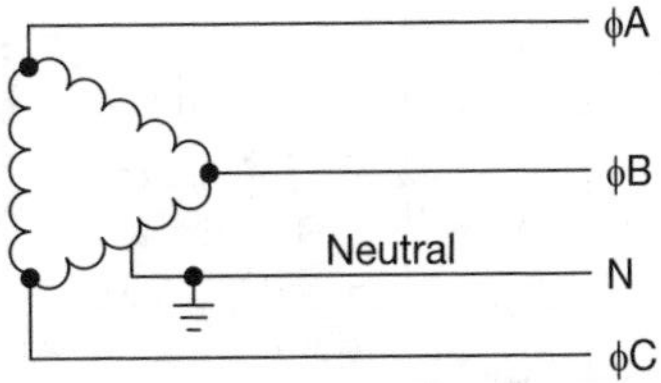

Three-Phase Delta, Four-Wire

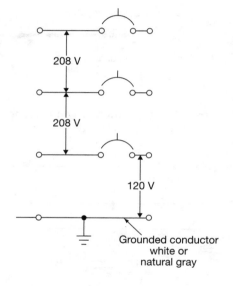

4-Wire System With a Neutral

VOLTAGE RELATIONSHIP ON GROUNDED 4-WIRE SYSTEMS

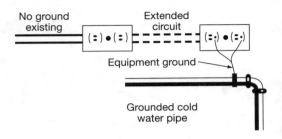

No ground existing

Extended circuit

Equipment ground

Grounded cold water pipe

Grounding Equipment on an Existing Circuit That is Not Grounded

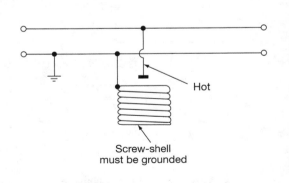

Hot

Screw-shell must be grounded

Grounding of a Screw-Shell Base

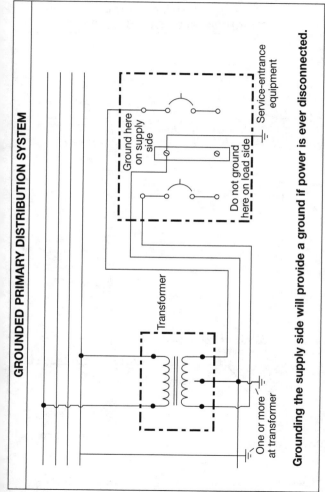

GROUNDED PRIMARY DISTRIBUTION SYSTEM

Transformer

Service-entrance equipment

Ground here on supply side

Do not ground here on load side

One or more at transformer

Grounding the supply side will provide a ground if power is ever disconnected.

GROUNDING A TYPICAL
OVERHEAD ELECTRICAL SERVICE

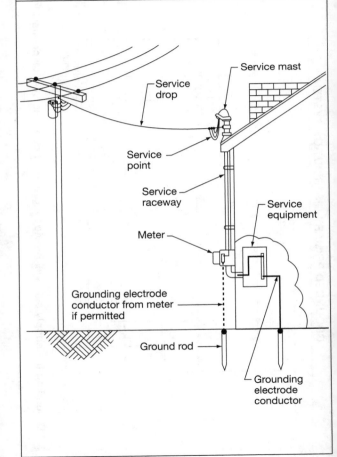

Service drop

Service mast

Service point

Service raceway

Service equipment

Meter

Grounding electrode conductor from meter if permitted

Ground rod

Grounding electrode conductor

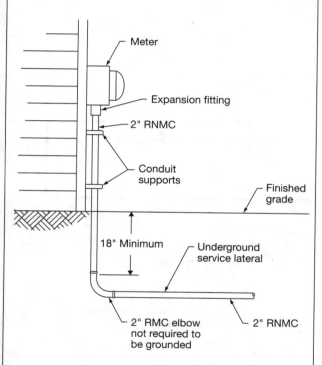

GROUNDING A TYPICAL NONMETALLIC UNDERGROUND SERVICE RACEWAY

Meter

Expansion fitting

2" RNMC

Conduit supports

Finished grade

18" Minimum

Underground service lateral

2" RMC elbow not required to be grounded

2" RNMC

Metal elbows installed in nonmetallic raceways are not required to be grounded when they are a minimum of 18" below the finished grade.

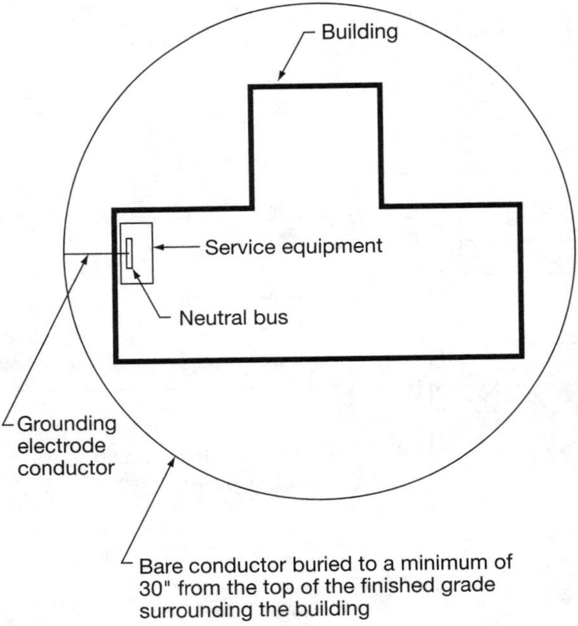

GROUNDING ELECTRODE SYSTEMS

Building

Service equipment

Neutral bus

Grounding electrode conductor

Bare conductor buried to a minimum of 30" from the top of the finished grade surrounding the building

**Ground Ring
(also called Counterpoise)**

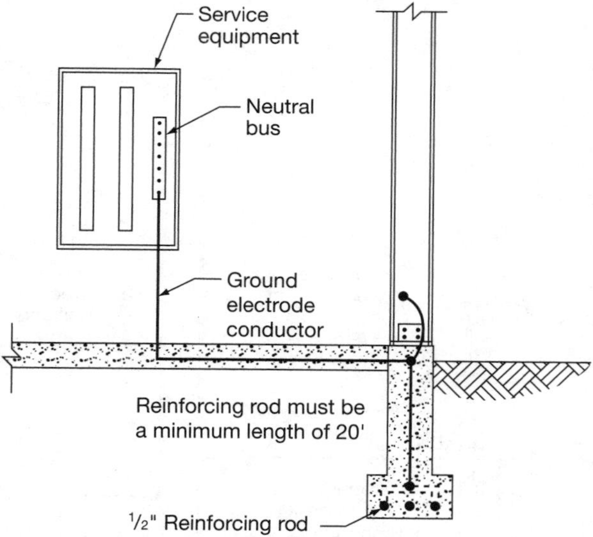

Service equipment

Neutral bus

Ground electrode conductor

Reinforcing rod must be a minimum length of 20'

$1/2$" Reinforcing rod

Concrete-Encased Electrode

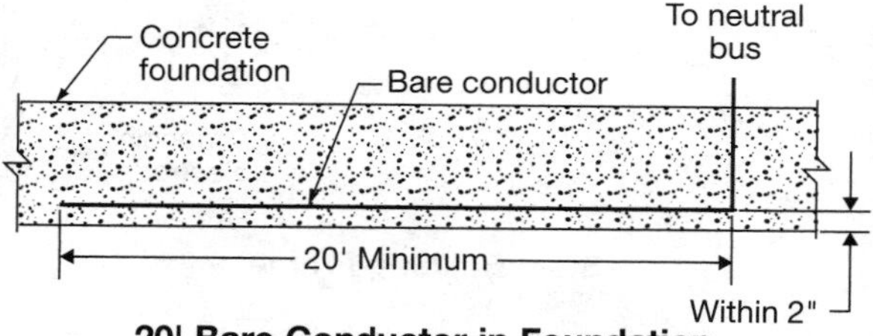

Concrete foundation

Bare conductor

To neutral bus

20' Minimum

Within 2"

20' Bare Conductor in Foundation

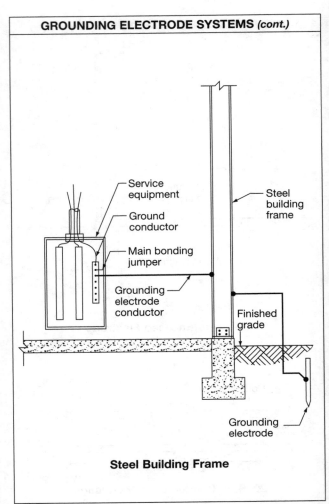

Steel Building Frame

Grounded conductor terminal bar (neutral)

Panel

Main bonding jumper

Grounding electrode conductors

Water meter

Service raceway

Bonding jumper

5'

Grounding electrode conductor shall terminate within 5' of metal water pipe entering building

Metal Underground Water Piping

GROUNDING AND BONDING A TYPICAL SERVICE ENTRANCE

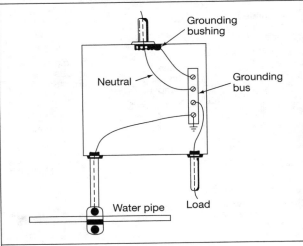

Grounding bushing

Neutral

Grounding bus

Water pipe

Load

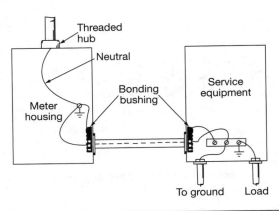

Threaded hub

Neutral

Meter housing

Bonding bushing

Service equipment

To ground

Load

PROPER BONDING OF A WATER METER

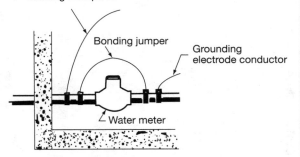

If grounding electrode conductor is on street side of water meter, bonding is required

Bonding jumper

Grounding electrode conductor

Water meter

Leave bonding jumper long enough so that it will not have to be removed in meter replacement

UFER GROUND

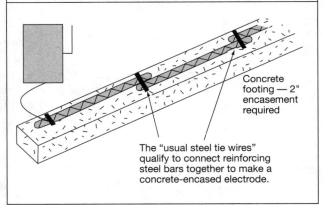

Concrete footing — 2" encasement required

The "usual steel tie wires" qualify to connect reinforcing steel bars together to make a concrete-encased electrode.

GROUNDING AN OUTDOOR ANTENNA

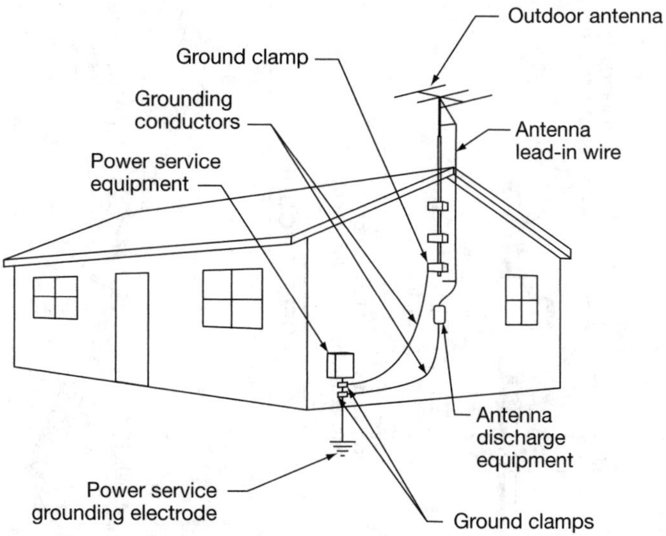

- Outdoor antenna
- Antenna lead-in wire
- Antenna discharge equipment
- Ground clamps
- Ground clamp
- Grounding conductors
- Power service equipment
- Power service grounding electrode

GROUNDING SEPARATELY DERIVED SYSTEMS IN MULTIPLE FLOOR BUILDINGS

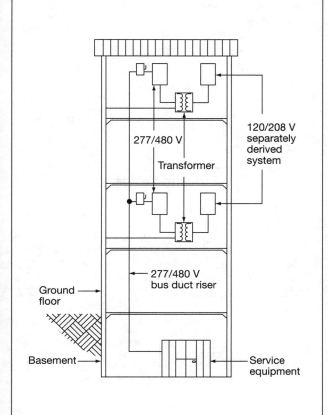

120/208 V separately derived system

277/480 V

Transformer

277/480 V bus duct riser

Ground floor

Basement

Service equipment

MAIN BONDING JUMPERS

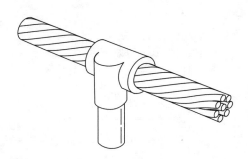

Exothermic Welds

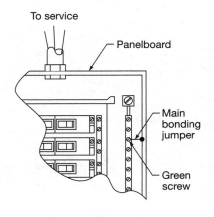

To service

Panelboard

Main bonding jumper

Green screw

Green Screw

BONDING SERVICE EQUIPMENT METHODS

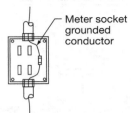

Meter socket grounded conductor

Grounded Service Conductor

Internal Threadless Connections

Internal Threaded Connections

Bonding bushing

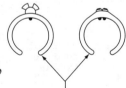

Bonding and grounding wedges

Bonding locknut

Other Devices

BONDING JUMPERS FOR GROUNDING EQUIPMENT CONDUCTOR RACEWAYS

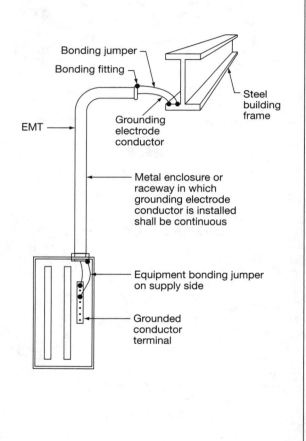

Bonding jumper

Bonding fitting

Steel building frame

EMT

Grounding electrode conductor

Metal enclosure or raceway in which grounding electrode conductor is installed shall be continuous

Equipment bonding jumper on supply side

Grounded conductor terminal

INSTALLING EQUIPMENT BONDING JUMPERS

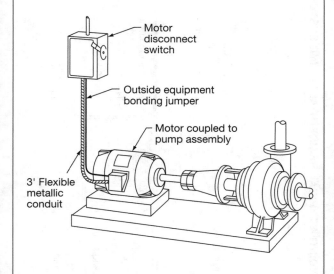

Motor disconnect switch

Outside equipment bonding jumper

Motor coupled to pump assembly

3' Flexible metallic conduit

Six feet maximum length on outside and routed with raceway.

Installed inside or outside of the raceway or enclosure.

GROUNDING A TYPICAL RESIDENTIAL WIRING SYSTEM

Nonmetallic cable

Neutral

Bonding screw

Neutral bus bar

Hot

Nonmetallic fitting

Neutral

Ground wire

Ground bus bar

Hot from meter

Main disconnect

Hot

Metal conduit fitting

Neutral

Bonding screw

Ground wire to cold water pipe and/or ground rod

3-28

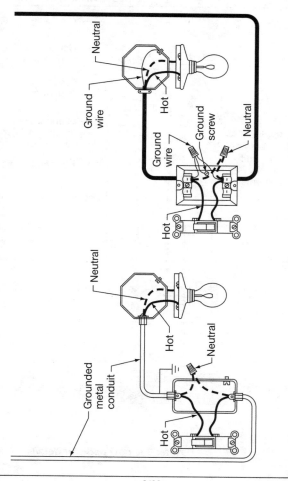

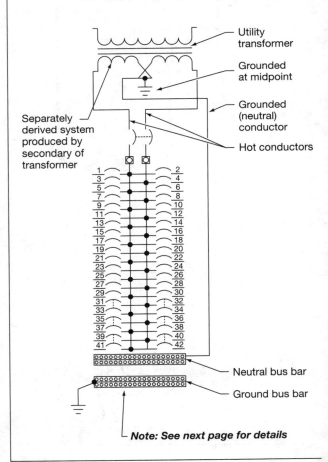

GROUNDING A TYPICAL

Utility transformer

Grounded at midpoint

Grounded (neutral) conductor

Hot conductors

Separately derived system produced by secondary of transformer

1	2
3	4
5	6
7	8
9	10
11	12
13	14
15	16
17	18
19	20
21	22
23	24
25	26
27	28
29	30
31	32
33	34
35	36
37	38
39	40
41	42

Neutral bus bar

Ground bus bar

Note: See next page for details

3-30

COMMERCIAL WIRING SYSTEM

Subpanel

Neutral bus

Ground bus

Isolated grounding system

Grounded conductor

Conduit ground

Equipment grounding conductor

Service entrance panel

Neutral bus

Ground bus

Conduit ground

Grounding electrode conductor

Service entrance grounding system

Main bonding jumper

3-31

LOW VOLTAGE SERVICE

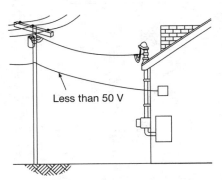

Less than 50 V

Installed as Overhead Conductor

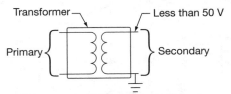

Transformer — Less than 50 V

Primary — Secondary

Ungrounded Transformer Supply

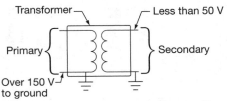

Transformer — Less than 50 V

Primary — Secondary

Over 150 V to ground

Transformer Supply Exceeds 150 V to Ground

GROUNDING A SIGNAL LOOP

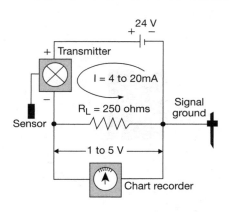

DEDICATED INSTRUMENTATION
SYSTEM GROUND BUS

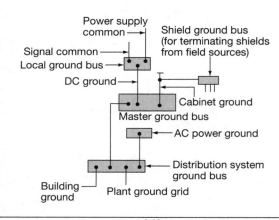

GROUND LOOPS MAY DEVELOP IN NON-ISOLATED SIGNAL LOOPS

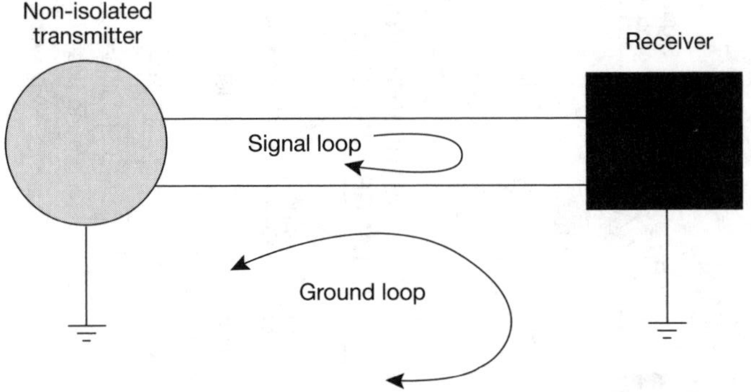

Receiver

Non-isolated transmitter

Signal loop

Ground loop

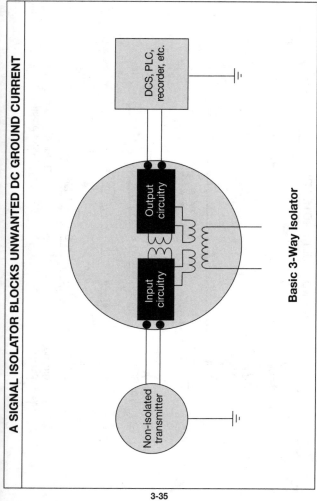

A SIGNAL ISOLATOR BLOCKS UNWANTED DC GROUND CURRENT

DCS, PLC, recorder, etc.

Output circuitry

Input circuitry

Non-isolated transmitter

Basic 3-Way Isolator

3-35

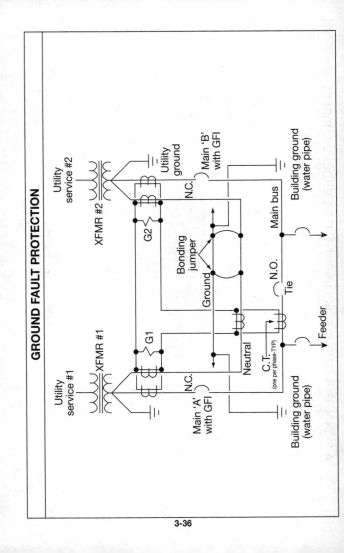

GROUND FAULT PROTECTION

GROUND FAULT PROTECTION (cont.)

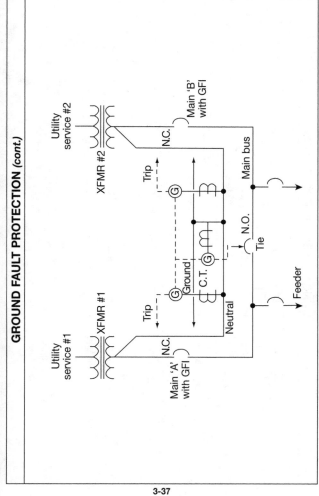

LIGHTNING AND SURGE PROTECTION

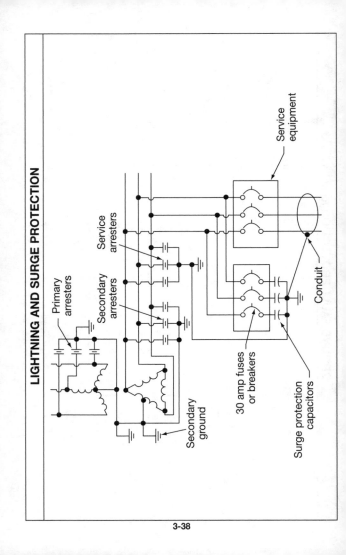

Primary arresters

Secondary arresters

Service arresters

Secondary ground

30 amp fuses or breakers

Surge protection capacitors

Service equipment

Conduit

CHAPTER 4
Motors and Controls

There are literally hundreds of different types of motors for thousands of different applications. Because of this, it is very important to understand the rules regarding the application and wiring of motors, as well as the control details. Generally, the concerns can be broken down into four categories:

1. Mechanical safety. This is to assure that the motors are not themselves a source of danger. For instance, we would not want to install open motors in areas where children could go. It would be simple for them to stick their fingers into the motor as it is operating, quickly injuring themselves, perhaps seriously. In the same manner, it is often necessary to put a clutch on a motor to avoid possible injury to a machine operator.

2. Mechanical stability and operations. Motors have a lot of mechanical stresses placed upon them. One of the primary forces is vibration, which has the unfortunate side effects of loosening bolts and screws. And not only the motor itself is subject to mechanical difficulties, but also the equipment that it operates and surrounding items.

3. Electrical safety. The first issue here is that motors do not become the source of an electrical shock or fault. Also that they do not cause problems to the electrical system on which they are installed.

4. Operational circuits. One last concern is that the circuits on which motors are installed can operate continually and correctly. Motors place unusual demands on electrical circuits. First of all, they can cause large starting currents. (Fully loaded motors can draw starting currents of 4 to 8 times their normal full load current; in some circumstances even higher.) They also put a lot of inductive reactance into electrical systems. And because of the high currents that some motors draw, they overheat electrical circuits more commonly than many other types of loads.

Suitable controllers are required for all motors. The simplest controller is just the branch-circuit protective device, which can be used as a controller for motors of 1/8 horsepower or less that are normally left running and cannot be damaged by overload or failure to start. Another simple "controller" is a simple cord-and-plug connection. This can be done for portable motors of 1/3 horsepower or less.

The important concern with motor starters is the ability to close and open the contacts that connect the motor to the source of electrical power. Unfortunately, it is not always possible to control the amount of mechanical load applied to the motor. Therefore, the motor may be overloaded, resulting in damage. For this reason, overload relays are added to the motor starter.

The goal is to protect the motor from overheating. The current drawn by the motor is a reasonably accurate measure of the load on the motor, and thus of its heating. Thus we call this protective device an overload device.

Most overloads today use a thermally responsive element. That is, the same current that goes to the motor coils (causing the motor to heat) also passes through the thermal elements of the overload relays.

The thermal element is connected mechanically to a normally closed contact. When an excessive current flows through the thermal element for a long enough time period, the contact is tripped open. This contact is connected in series with the control coil of the starter. When the contact opens, the starter coil is deenergized. In turn, the starter power contacts disconnect the motor from the line.

A motor can operate on a slight overload for a long period of time or at a higher overload for a short period of time. Overheating of the motor will not result in either case. Therefore, the overload heater element should be designed to have heat-storage characteristics similar to those of the motor. However, they should be just enough faster so that the relay will trip the normally closed relay contact before excessive heating occurs in the motor.

DELTA-WOUND MOTOR FOR USE ON 240/480 VOLTS

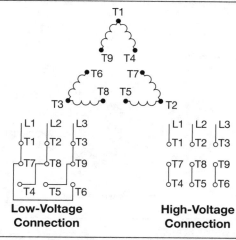

Low-Voltage Connection

High-Voltage Connection

WYE-WOUND MOTOR FOR USE ON 240/480 VOLTS

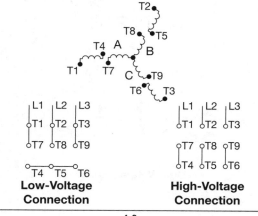

Low-Voltage Connection

High-Voltage Connection

SPLIT-PHASE MOTORS

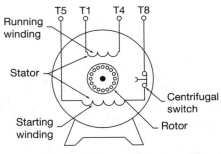

Single-Voltage Motor

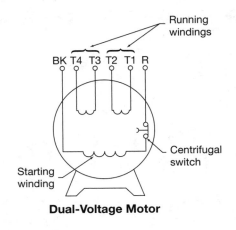

Dual-Voltage Motor

SPLIT-PHASE MOTOR ROTATION

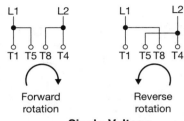

Forward rotation

Reverse rotation

Single-Voltage

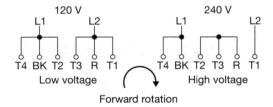

120 V — Low voltage

240 V — High voltage

Forward rotation

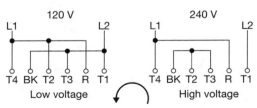

120 V — Low voltage

240 V — High voltage

Reverse rotation

Dual-Voltage

SINGLE-VOLTAGE, 3φ, WYE-CONNECTED MOTOR

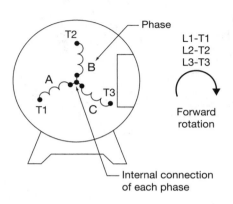

Phase

L1-T1
L2-T2
L3-T3

Forward rotation

Internal connection of each phase

SINGLE-VOLTAGE, 3φ, DELTA-CONNECTED MOTOR

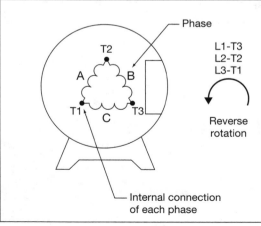

Phase

L1-T3
L2-T2
L3-T1

Reverse rotation

Internal connection of each phase

DUAL-VOLTAGE, 3φ, WYE-CONNECTED MOTORS

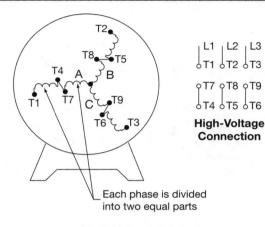

Each phase is divided
into two equal parts

High-Voltage Connection

L1	L2	L3
T1	T2	T3

T7	T8	T9
T4	T5	T6

High-Voltage (series)

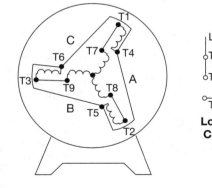

Low-Voltage Connection

L1	L2	L3
T1	T2	T3
T7	T8	T9

| T4 | T5 | T6 |

Low-Voltage (parallel)

4-7

DUAL-VOLTAGE, 3φ, DELTA-CONNECTED MOTORS

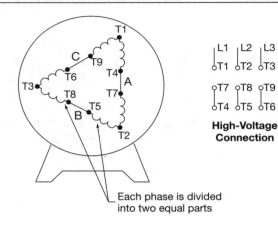

High-Voltage Connection

Each phase is divided into two equal parts

High-Voltage (series)

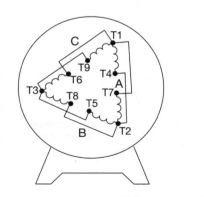

Low-Voltage Connection

Low-Voltage (parallel)

STAR-CONNECTED, POLYPHASE MOTOR

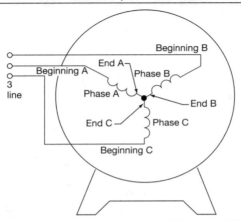

REVERSING THREE-PHASE MOTORS

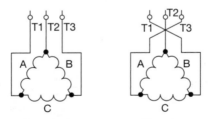

Forward   **Reverse**

Reversing direction is accomplished by interchanging any two of the three power lines. Although any two may be interchanged, the industry standard is to interchange L1 and L3. This is true for all 3ϕ motors including three, six, and nine lead wye- and delta-connected motors.

TWO-PHASE, AC MOTORS

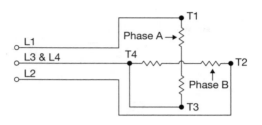

3-Wire
To reverse direction, interchange L1 and L2.

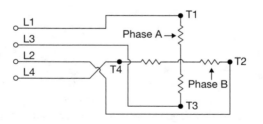

4-Wire
**To reverse direction, interchange the
leads in one phase.**

CONNECTIONS FOR A TWO-SPEED, CONSTANT HORSEPOWER, ONE WINDING MOTOR

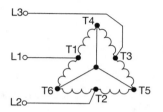

Low Speed

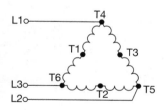

High Speed

Note: Torque decreases in the same ratio as speed increases maintaining constant horsepower.

CONNECTIONS FOR A TWO-SPEED, CONSTANT TORQUE, ONE WINDING MOTOR

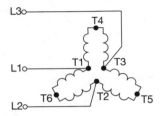

Low Speed

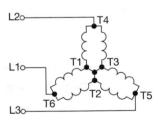

High Speed

Note: In a constant torque motor, the horsepower changes proportionally to the speed.

CONNECTIONS FOR A TWO-SPEED, VARIABLE TORQUE, ONE WINDING MOTOR

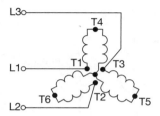

Low Speed

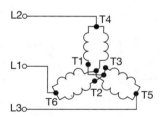

High Speed

Note: In a variable torque motor, the torque and the horsepower vary inversely with the speed.

CAPACITOR-START-CAPACITOR-RUN MOTOR

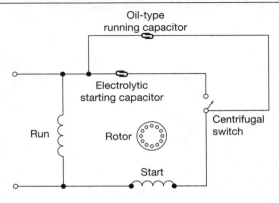

REVERSING A CAPACITOR-START MOTOR

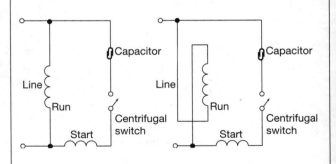

The reversal of a capacitor-start motor is accomplished by reversing the leads of the running winding.

CAPACITOR-START MOTOR VOLTAGE CONNECTIONS

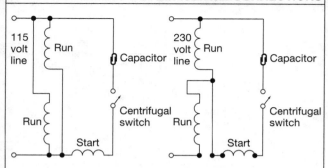

**Capacitor-start motor, first connected
across 115 volts and then across 230 volts.**

TWO-SPEED CAPACITOR MOTOR

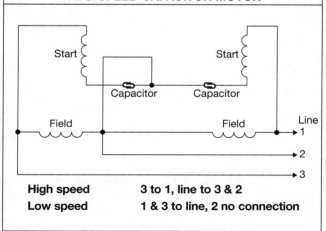

| High speed | 3 to 1, line to 3 & 2 |
| Low speed | 1 & 3 to line, 2 no connection |

WOUND-ROTOR MOTOR SCHEMATIC

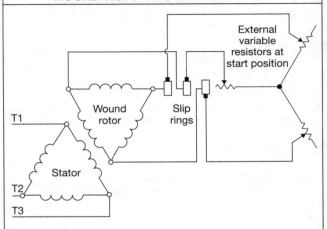

REVERSING SPLIT-PHASE MOTORS

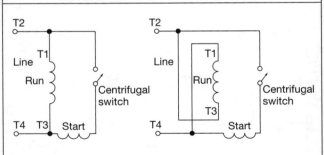

The reversal of a split-phase motor is accomplished by reversing the running winding leads.

TYPICAL MOTOR STARTER DIAGRAM

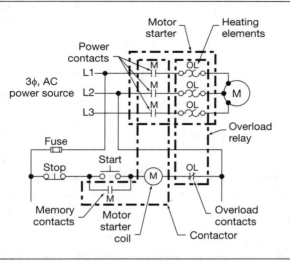

Motor starter

Heating elements

Power contacts

3φ, AC power source

L1
L2
L3

M
OL

Overload relay

Fuse

Stop
Start

Memory contacts

Motor starter coil

Overload contacts

Contactor

STEP-DOWN TRANSFORMER MOTOR CONTROL

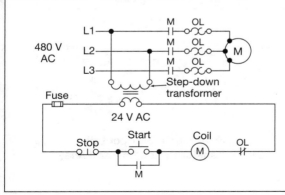

480 V AC

L1
L2
L3

M   OL

Step-down transformer

Fuse

24 V AC

Stop   Start   Coil

M   OL

M

4-17

MOTOR CONTROL CIRCUITS

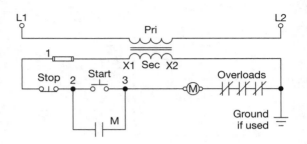

Low-voltage motor control using a transformer.

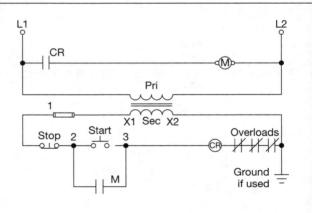

**Low-voltage motor control
using a transformer and control relay.**

MOTOR CONTROL CIRCUITS *(cont.)*

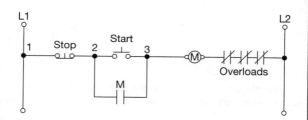

**Magnetic three-phase starter
with one start-stop station.**

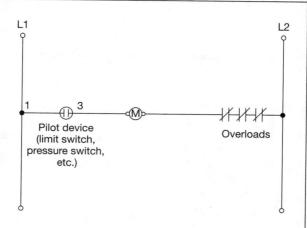

Maintained-contact control.

MOTOR CONTROL CIRCUITS *(cont.)*

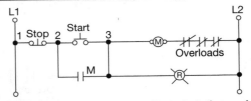

Magnetic starter with one stop-start station and a pilot lamp which burns to indicate that the motor is running.

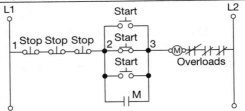

Magnetic starter with three stop-start stations.

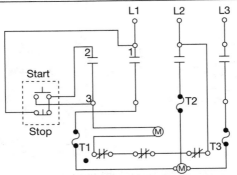

Diagrammatic representation of a magnetic three-phase starter with one start-stop station.

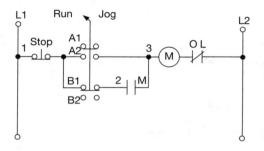

Jogging using a selector push button.

Magnetic starter with a plugging switch.

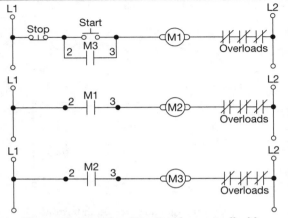

**Three motors simultaneously controlled by
one stop-start station; if one overload device trips,
all three motors will stop running.**

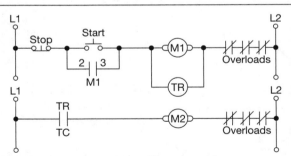

**Two magnetic starters controlled by one
start-stop station; a starting-time delay
device between the two motors.**

MOTOR CONTROL CIRCUITS *(cont.)*

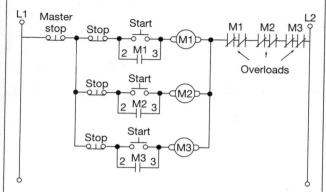

**Three separately started motors stopped
by one master stop station or stopped if
one overload device is tripped.**

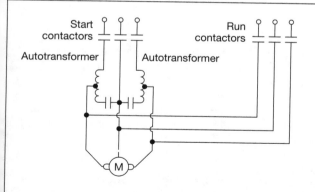

Starting compensator, with start and run contacts.

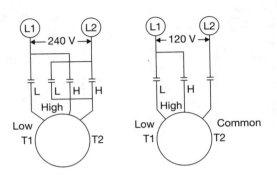

**Wiring diagram for a two-speed,
single-phase 240 V motor.**

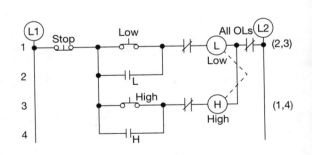

Basic two-speed motor control circuit.

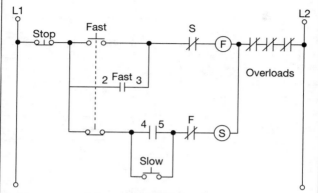

**A two-speed, three-phase,
squirrel-cage motor starter.**

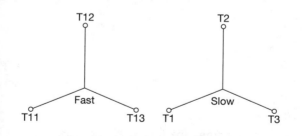

Motor Windings

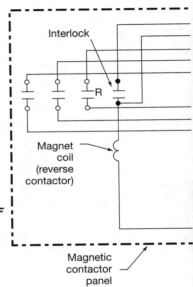

Interlock

R

Magnet
coil
(reverse
contactor)

Note:
Contactors R and F
are mechanically
interlocked

Magnetic
contactor
panel

**An across-the-line reversing type
starter controlling a three-phase motor.**

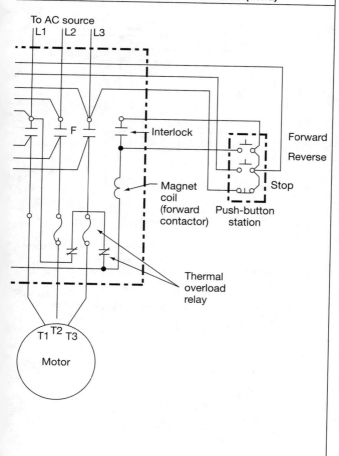

To AC source
L1 L2 L3

F

Interlock

Forward

Reverse

Stop

Magnet coil (forward contactor)

Push-button station

Thermal overload relay

T1 T2 T3

Motor

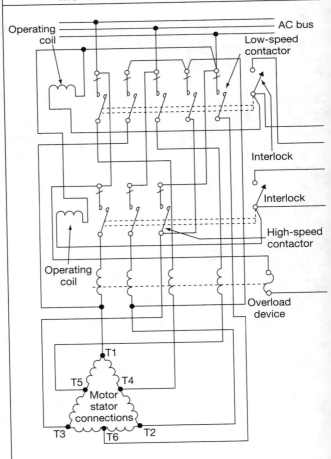

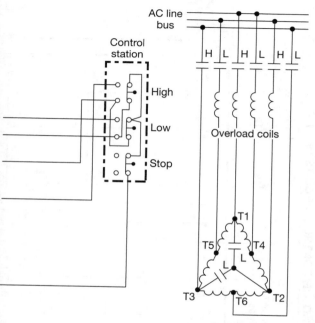

A two-speed AC motor with push-button control.

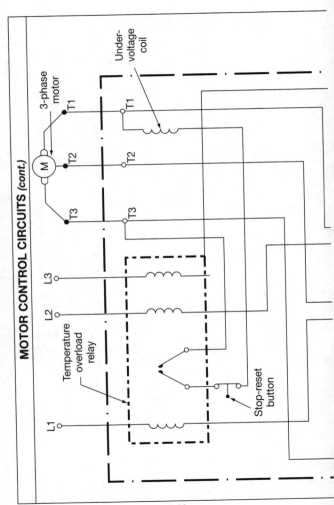

MOTOR CONTROL CIRCUITS (cont.)

3-phase motor

Under-voltage coil

Temperature overload relay

Stop-reset button

4-30

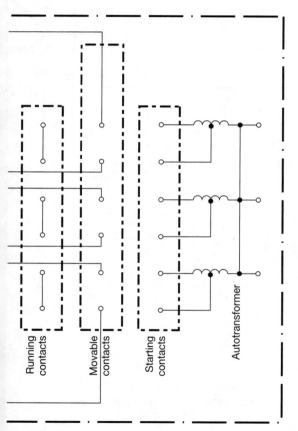

Manual-type starting compensator.

Running contacts

Movable contacts

Starting contacts

Autotransformer

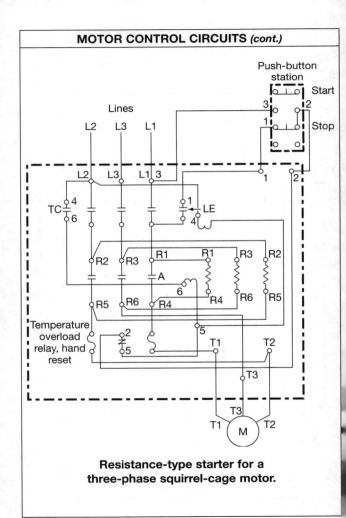

Resistance-type starter for a three-phase squirrel-cage motor.

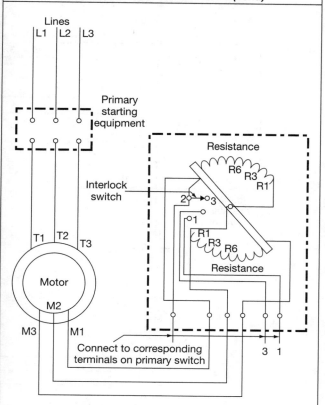

**Diagram of a faceplate starter
for a wound-rotor induction motor.**

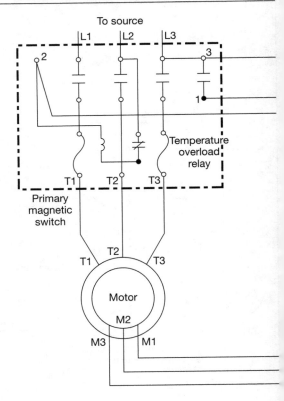

To source

L1 L2 L3

2   3

1

Temperature
overload
relay

T1 T2 T3

Primary
magnetic
switch

T1   T2   T3

Motor

M2

M3   M1

Secondary speed-regulating rheostat and a

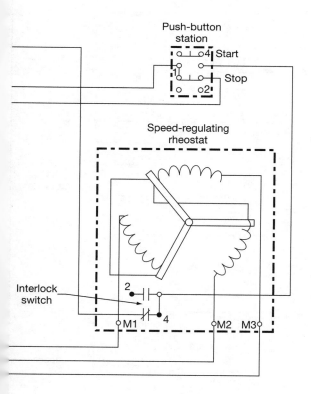

primary magnetic switch for a wound-rotor motor.

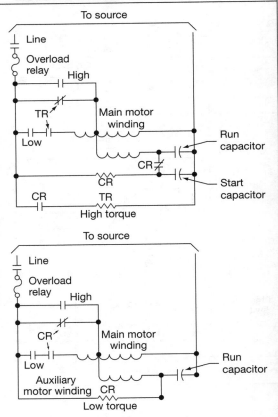

Starting and running circuits of low-torque and high-torque adjustable-speed capacitor motors with tapped main windings.

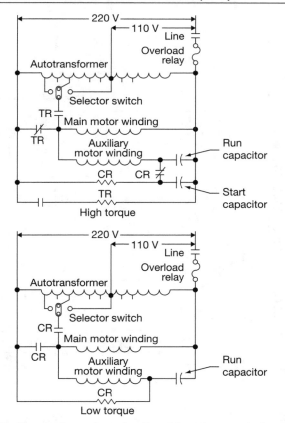

Starting and running circuits of low-torque and
high-torque adjustable-speed capacitor motors with
manually operated transformer speed regulator.

MOTOR CONTROL CIRCUITS (cont.)

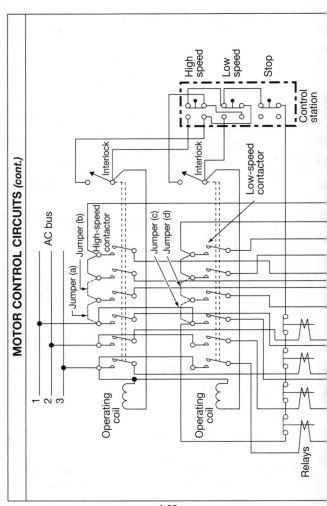

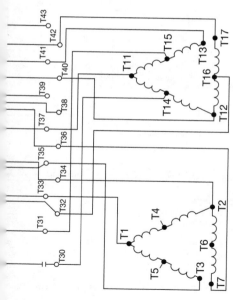

The control arrangement for an AC multispeed motor.

Motor stator connectors

T30 T31 T32 T33 T34 T35 T36 T37 T38 T39 T40 T41 T42 T43

T1 T4 T2 T5 T3 T6 T7

T11 T15 T13 T17 T14 T16 T12

4-39

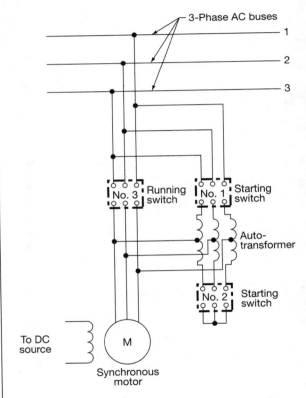

- 3-Phase AC buses
  - 1
  - 2
  - 3

No. 3 Running switch

No. 1 Starting switch

Autotransformer

No. 2 Starting switch

To DC source

M

Synchronous motor

An autotransformer starter for a synchronous motor.

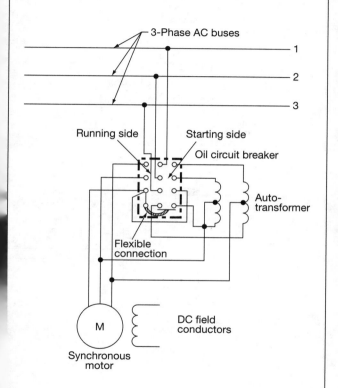

A reduced-voltage starter for a synchronous motor.

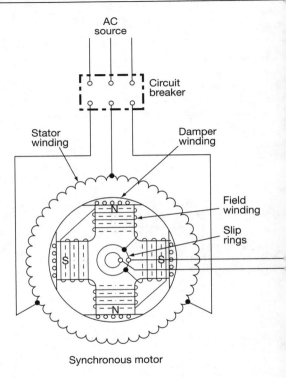

AC
source

Circuit
breaker

Stator
winding

Damper
winding

Field
winding

Slip
rings

Synchronous motor

Connections of a synchronous motor and exciter with the

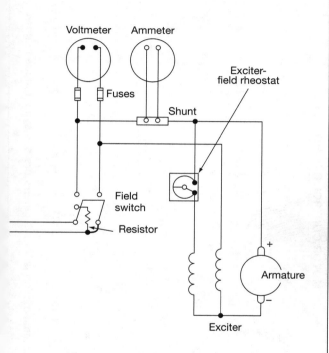

exciter-field rheostat, field switch, and exciter-field meters.

MOTOR CONTROL CIRCUITS *(cont.)*

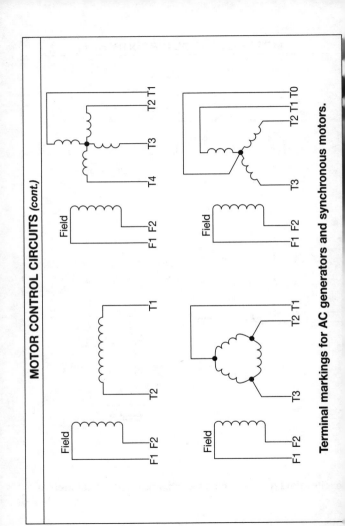

Terminal markings for AC generators and synchronous motors.

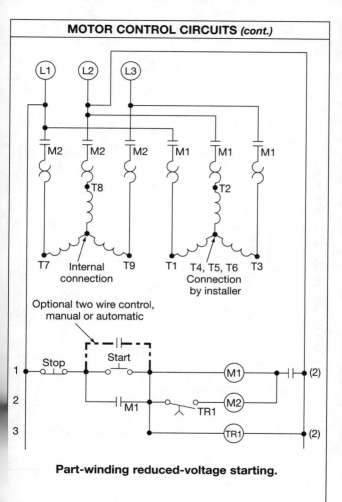

Part-winding reduced-voltage starting.

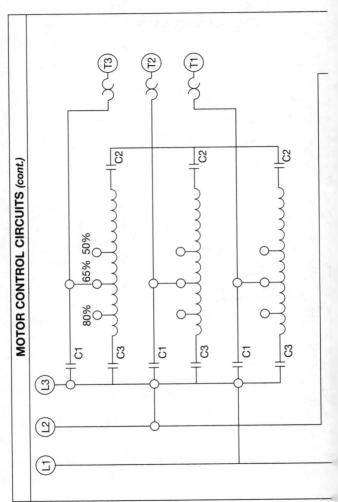

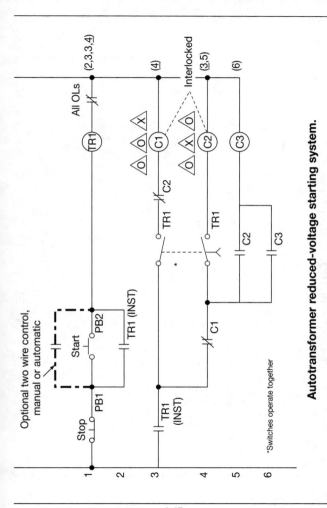

Autotransformer reduced-voltage starting system.

4-47

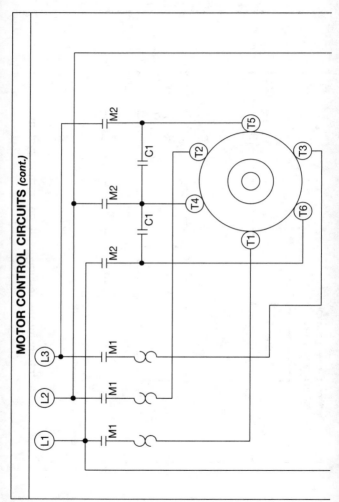

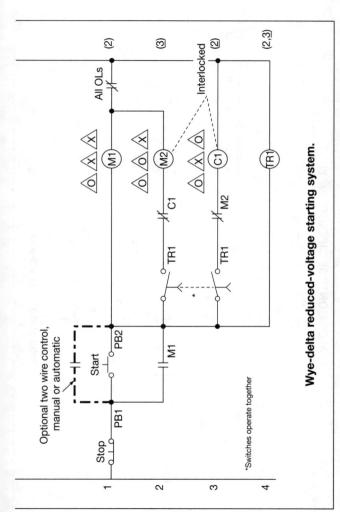

Wye-delta reduced-voltage starting system.

4-49

MOTOR CONTROL CIRCUITS (cont.)

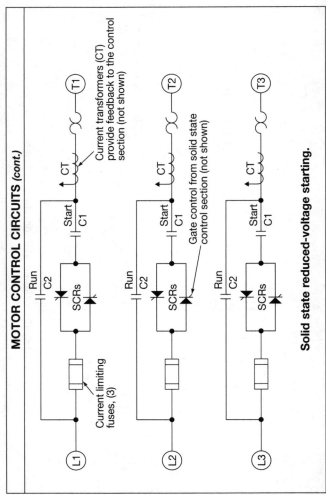

Current transformers (CT) provide feedback to the control section (not shown)

Gate control from solid state control section (not shown)

Current limiting fuses, (3)

Solid state reduced-voltage starting.

MOTOR CONTROL CIRCUITS *(cont.)*

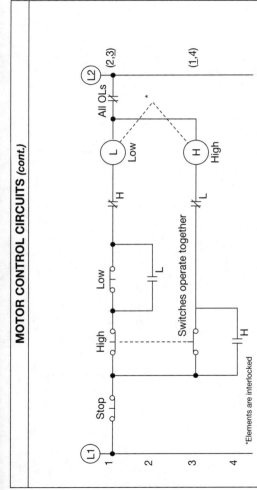

Changing from low speed to high speed without stopping the motor.

4-51

MOTOR CONTROL CIRCUITS *(cont.)*

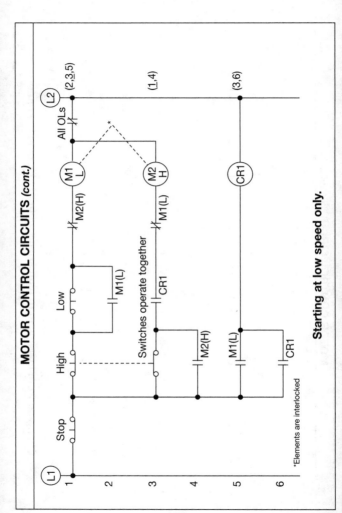

Starting at low speed only.

*Elements are interlocked

4-52

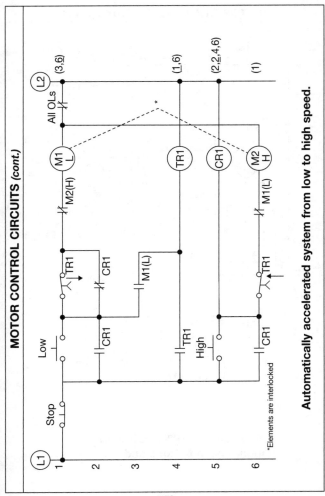

MOTOR CONTROL CIRCUITS (cont.)

Automatically accelerated system from low to high speed.

*Elements are interlocked

4-53

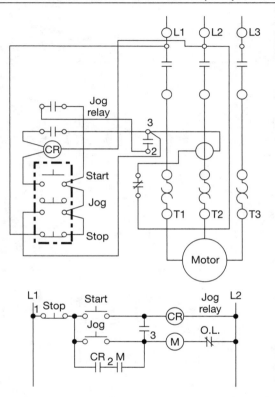

Separate "START-STOP-JOG" with standard push buttons and a JOG relay.

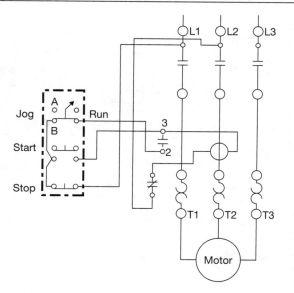

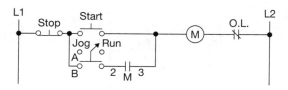

**Combined "START, JOG" and separate "STOP"
with selector switch. Jogging with a selector switch.**

MOTOR CONTROL CIRCUITS (cont.)

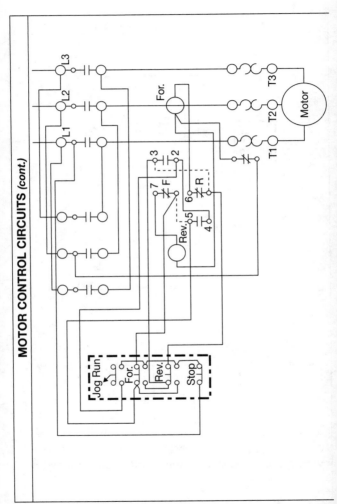

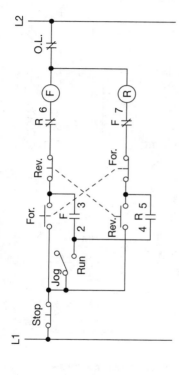

**Starting, Stopping and Jogging in either direction.
Jogging controlled through a Jogging selector switch.**

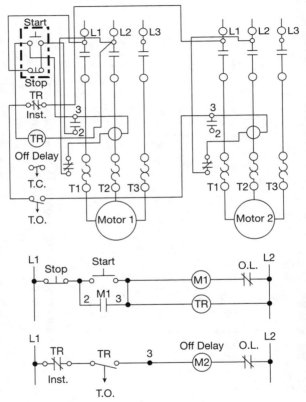

**Sequence Control of Two Motors — one to
start and run for a short time after the other stops.**

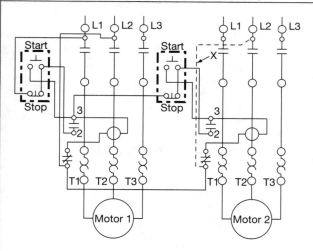

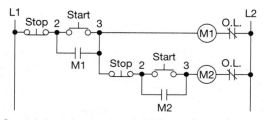

Control circuit is connected only to the lines of Motor 1.

**Starters arranged for sequence
control of a conveyor system.**

DC SERIES-WOUND MOTOR

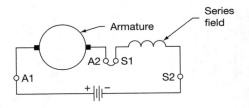

DC SHUNT-WOUND MOTOR

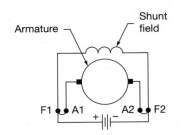

DC COMPOUND-WOUND MOTOR

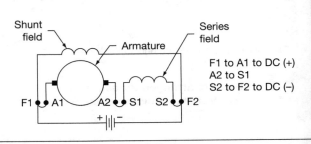

F1 to A1 to DC (+)
A2 to S1
S2 to F2 to DC (–)

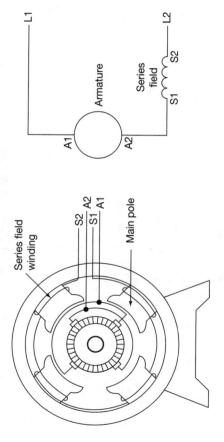

Connections for a series-wound DC motor.

DC MOTOR CONNECTIONS (cont.)

Shunt-wound DC motor with interpoles.

The interpoles (commutating poles) are in series with the armature so that their field strength will be proportional to the load on the motor.

DC MOTOR CONNECTIONS *(cont.)*

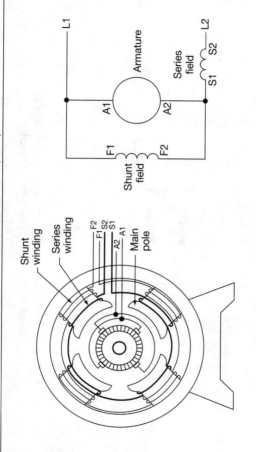

Cumulatively compound-wound DC motor.

DC MOTOR CONNECTIONS *(cont.)*

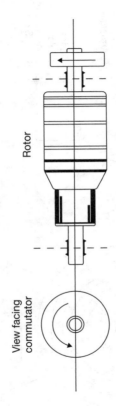

View facing commutator

Rotor

Standard direction of rotation is counterclockwise when facing commutator end of motor.

DC MOTOR CONNECTIONS (cont.)

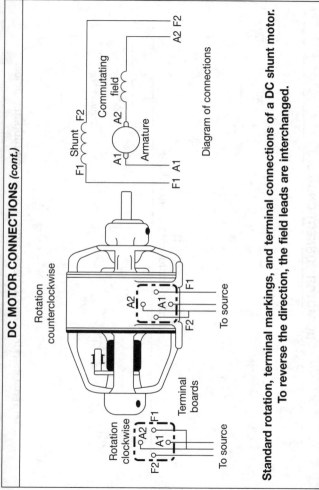

Rotation counterclockwise

A2 A1 F1

F2

To source

Rotation clockwise

A2 F1

A1

F2

Terminal boards

To source

Shunt F2

F1

Commutating field

A2 A1

Armature

A2 F2

F1 A1

Diagram of connections

Standard rotation, terminal markings, and terminal connections of a DC shunt motor. To reverse the direction, the field leads are interchanged.

DC MOTOR CONNECTIONS (cont.)

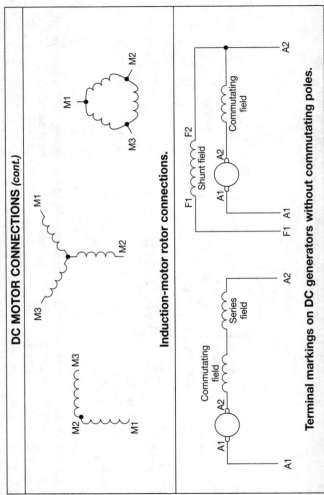

Induction-motor rotor connections.

Terminal markings on DC generators without commutating poles.

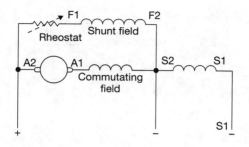

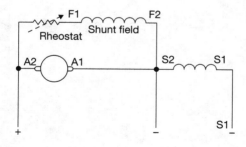

Terminal markings on DC compound generators.

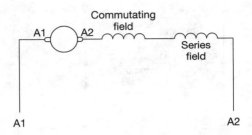

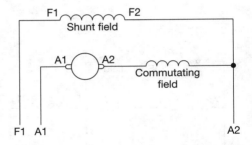

**Terminal markings on nonreversing
commutating-pole types of DC motors.**

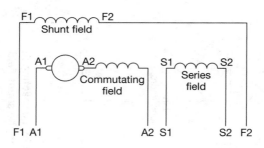

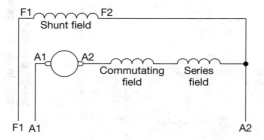

**Terminal markings on compound
commutating-pole types of DC motors.**

DC MOTOR CONTROL CIRCUITS

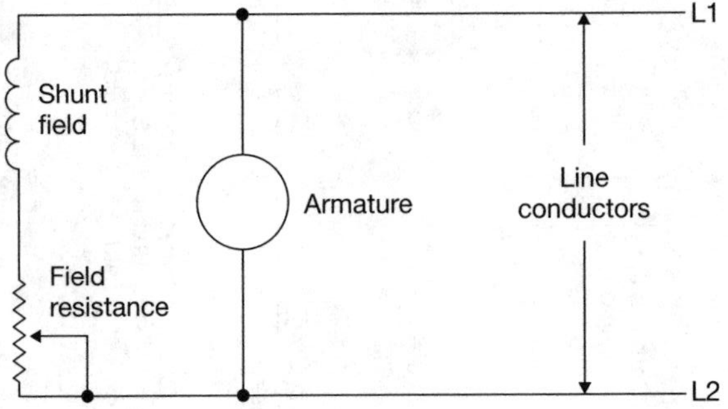

L1

L2

Line conductors

Armature

Shunt field

Field resistance

Speed control for a DC motor by connecting a variable resistance in series with the shunt field.

DC MOTOR CONTROL CIRCUITS *(cont.)*

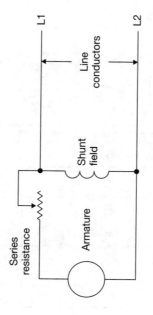

L1

L2

Line
conductors

Shunt
field

Series
resistance

Armature

Speed control for a DC motor by connecting a variable resistance in series with the armature.

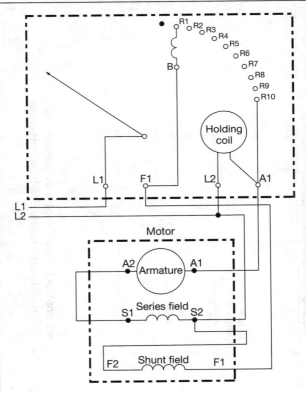

Connections between a compound DC motor and a faceplate starter.

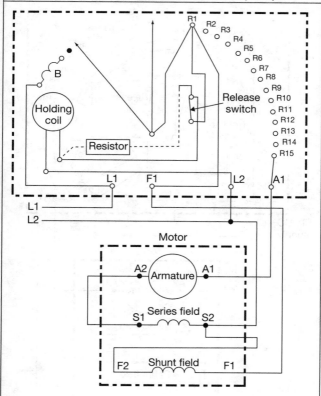

DC MOTOR CONTROL CIRCUITS *(cont.)*

R1 R2 R3 R4 R5 R6 R7 R8 R9 R10 R11 R12 R13 R14 R15

B

Holding coil

Release switch

Resistor

L1 F1 L2 A1

L1
L2

Motor

A2 Armature A1

Series field S1 S2

F2 Shunt field F1

Connections between a compound DC motor and a speed-regulating faceplate starter.

4-73

DC MOTOR CONTROL CIRCUITS *(cont.)*

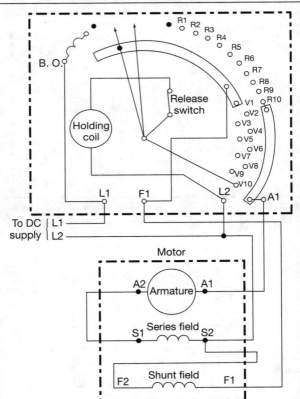

Connections between a compound DC motor and a faceplate starter used also for speed control.

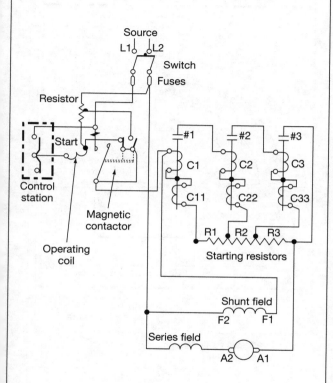

Counter-emf DC motor starter.

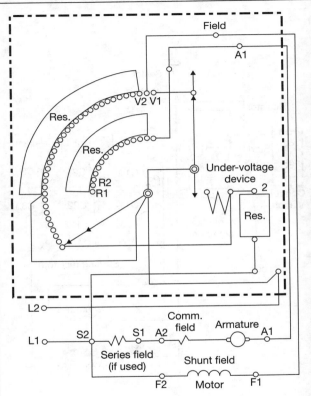

DC shunt motor speed-regulating rheostat for starting and speed control by field control.

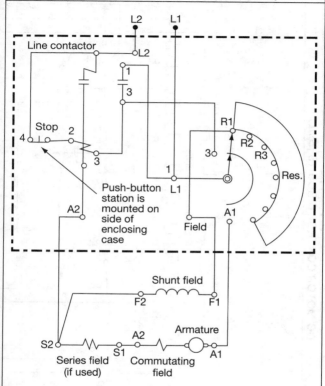

DC speed-regulating rheostat control for shunt or compound-wound motors with contactors and push-button station control.

DC MOTOR CONTROL CIRCUITS (cont.)

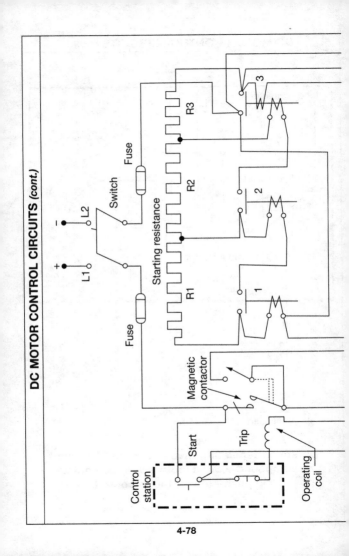

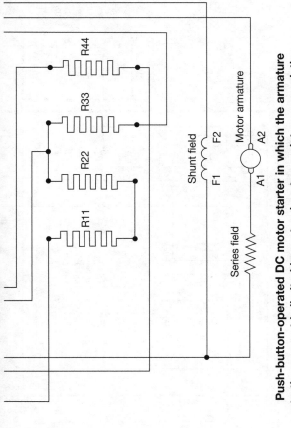

Push-button-operated DC motor starter in which the armature starting current is limited by a step-by-step resistance regulation.

DC MOTOR CONTROL CIRCUITS (cont.)

Front view

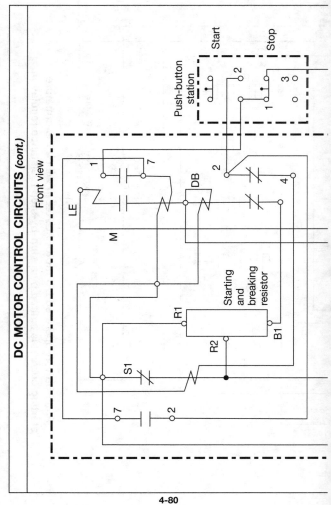

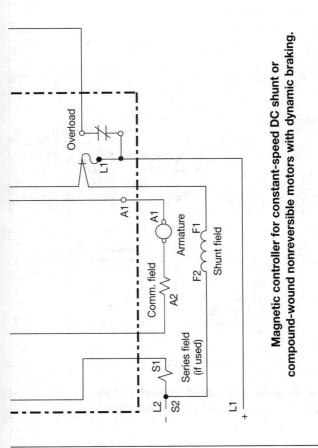

Magnetic controller for constant-speed DC shunt or compound-wound nonreversible motors with dynamic braking.

Overload

L1

A1

A1

Armature

Comm. field

A2

F1

Shunt field

F2

Series field
(if used)

S1

S2

L2
−

L1
+

4-81

DC MOTOR CONTROL CIRCUITS *(cont.)*

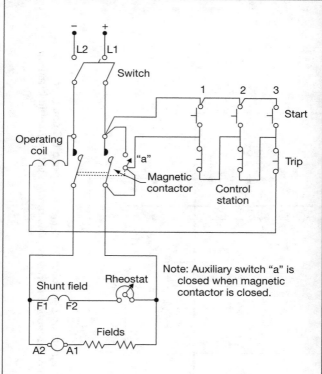

Note: Auxiliary switch "a" is closed when magnetic contactor is closed.

Magnetically operated DC motor starter with three push-button control stations.

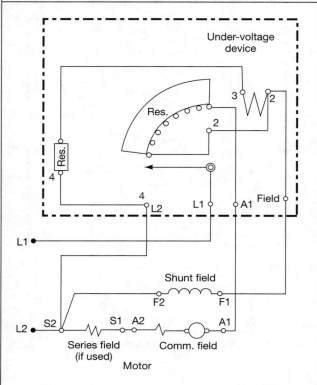

DC speed-regulating rheostat control for shunt or compound-wound motors without a contactor.

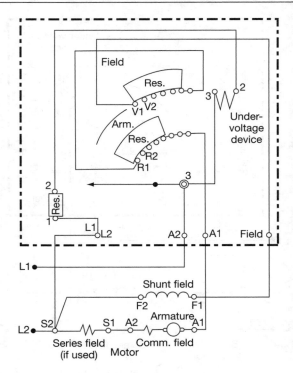

**DC speed-regulating rheostat control for
shunt or compound-wound motors; regulating
duty — 50% speed reduction by armature control
and 25% increase by field control.**

CHAPTER 5
Transformers

Transformers are devices that transform electrical energy from one circuit to another, usually at different levels of current and voltage, but at the same frequency. This is done through electromagnetic induction, in which the circuits never physically touch. The transformer is made of one or more coils of wire wrapped around a laminated iron core.

Transformer Installation

The requirements for installing and connecting transformers are detailed in Article 450 of the National Electrical Code (NEC). Per this article, the term transformer refers to a single transformer, whether it be single phase or polyphase.

Transformers *operating at over 600 volts* must have protective devices for both the primary and secondary of the transformer, sized according to Table 450-3(a)(1) of the NEC.

Transformers *rated 600 volts or less* can be protected by an overcurrent protective device on the primary side only, which must be rated at least 125 percent of the transformer's rated primary current.

Transformers *operating at less than 600 volts* are allowed to have overcurrent protection in the secondary only, which must be sized at 125 percent of the rated secondary current, if the feeder overcurrent device is rated at no more than 250 percent of the transformer's rated primary current.

Transformers *with thermal overload devices in the primary side* do not require additional protection in the primary side unless the feeder overcurrent device is more than six times the primary's rated current (for transformers with 6 percent impedance or less), or four times primary current (for transformers with between 6 and 10 percent impedance).

Potential transformers must have primary fuses.

Autotransformers rated 600 volts or less must be protected by an overcurrent protective device in each ungrounded input conductor, which must be rated at least 125 percent of the rated input current.

SINGLE-PHASE TRANSFORMER CIRCUITS

Series-Connected Winding for 3-Wire Service

Primary side — 2400 V

Secondary side — Neutral wire grounded — 120 V — 120 V — 240 V

Parallel-Connected Winding

Primary side — 2400 V

Secondary side — 120 V

Series-Connected Winding

Primary side — 2400 V

Two equal sections — 120 V — 120 V — 240 V

Secondary side

SINGLE-PHASE TRANSFORMER CONNECTIONS

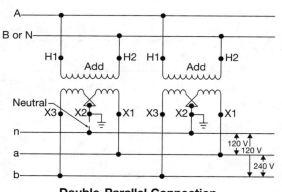

Double-Parallel Connection

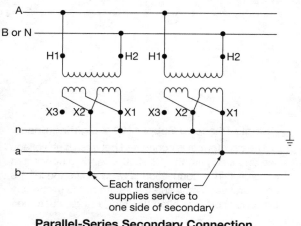

Parallel-Series Secondary Connection

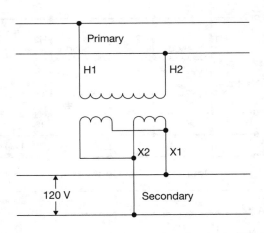

Single-Phase to Supply 120 V Lighting Load

The transformer is connected between high voltage line and load with the 120/240 V winding connected in parallel. This connection is used where the load is comparatively small and the length of the secondary circuit is short. It is often used for a single customer.

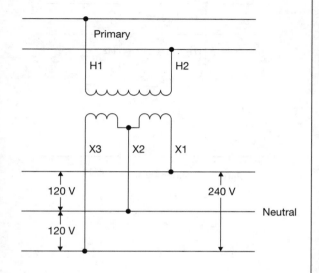

Single-Phase to Supply 120/240 V
3-Wire Lighting and Power Load

Here the 120/240 V winding is connected in series
and the mid-point brought out, making it possible to
serve both 120 and 240 V loads simultaneously. This
connection is used in most urban distribution circuits.

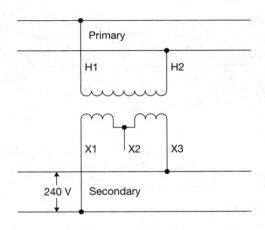

Primary

H1   H2

X1   X2   X3

240 V   Secondary

Single-Phase for Power

In this case the 120/240 V winding is connected in series serving 240 V on a two-wire system. This connection is used for small industrial applications.

TWO-PHASE TRANSFORMER CONNECTIONS

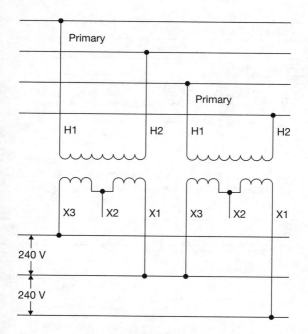

Two-Phase Connections

This connection consists merely of two single-phase transformers operated 90° out of phase. For a three-wire secondary as shown, the common wire must carry 32 times the load current. In some cases, a four-wire or a five-wire secondary may be used.

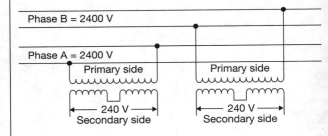

The most commonly used 2φ connection consists of two 1φ transformers connected for 2φ, four-wire circuits on both the primary and secondary sides.

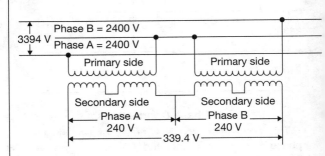

Two 1φ transformers are connected with one side of the primaries connected to the same line and the other side of the primaries connected to different lines when a 2φ, 3-wire circuit is required.

THREE-PHASE AC CIRCUITS

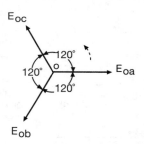

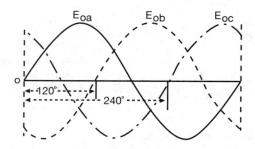

Sine waves are actually an oscillograph trace taken at any point in a three-phase system. (Each voltage or current wave actually comes from a separate wire but are shown for comparison on common base). There are 120° between each voltage. At any instant the algebraic sum (measured up and down from centerline) of these three voltages is zero. When one voltage is zero, the other two are 86.6% maximum and have opposite signs.

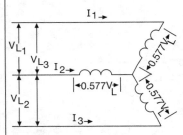

Wye-Connection

Consider the three windings as primary of transformer. Current in all windings equals line current, but volts across windings = 0.577 × line volts.

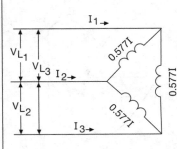

Delta Connection

Winding voltages equal line voltages, but currents split up so 0.577 I_{line} flows through windings.

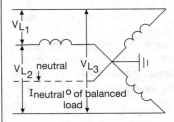

Four-Wire System

Most popular secondary distribution setup. V_1 is usually 208 V which feeds small power loads. Lighting loads at 120 V tap from any line to neutral.

THREE-PHASE TRANSFORMER CONNECTIONS

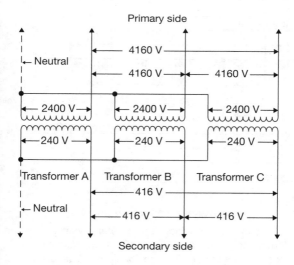

Primary side

Neutral

4160 V

4160 V — 4160 V

2400 V — 2400 V — 2400 V

240 V — 240 V — 240 V

Transformer A   Transformer B   Transformer C

416 V

416 V — 416 V

Neutral

Secondary side

4160 V

A   B

4160 V   4160 V

C

Primary side

416 V

a   b

416 V   416 V

c

Secondary side

Wye-to-Wye Connection

Three 1φ transformers may be connected in a wye-to-wye connection to form a 3φ transformer.

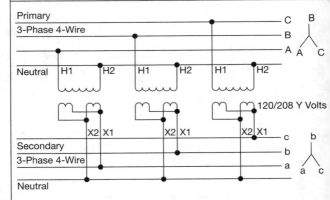

Wye-to-Wye for Lighting and Power

A system on which the primary voltage was increased from 2400 V to 4160 V to increase the potential capacity. The previously delta connected distribution transformers are now connected from line to neutral. The secondaries are connected in wye. The primary neutral is connected to the neutral of the supply voltage through a metallic conductor and carried with the phase conductor to minimize telephone interference. If the neutral of the transformer is isolated from the system neutral, an unstable condition results at the transformer neutral caused primarily by third harmonic voltages. If the transformer neutral is connected to ground, the possibility of telephone interference is enhanced and a possibility of resonance between the line capacitance to ground and the magnetizing impedance of the transformer.

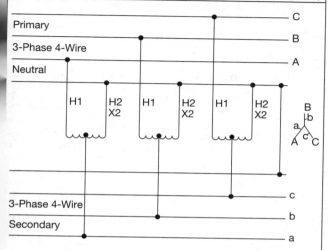

Wye-to-Wye Autotransformers for Supplying Power From a Three-Phase Four-Wire System

When ratio of transformation from primary to secondary voltage is small, the best way of stepping down voltage is using autotransformers. It is necessary that the neutral of the autotransformer bank be connected to the system neutral.

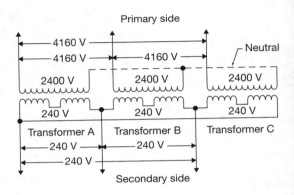

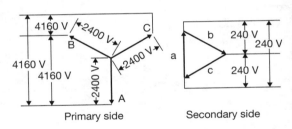

Wye-to-Delta Connection

A wye-to-delta connection permits 1φ and 3φ loads to be drawn simultaneously from the delta-connected secondary at the same voltage.

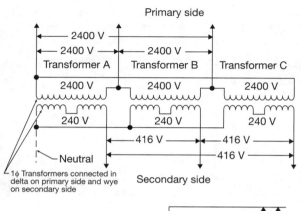

Primary side

2400 V

2400 V — 2400 V

Transformer A | Transformer B | Transformer C

2400 V | 2400 V | 2400 V

240 V | 240 V | 240 V

416 V — 416 V

416 V

Neutral

1φ Transformers connected in delta on primary side and wye on secondary side

Secondary side

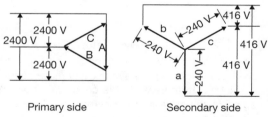

Primary side

Secondary side

Delta-to-Wye Connection

A 3φ delta-to-wye connection is often used for distribution where a four-wire secondary distribution circuit is required.

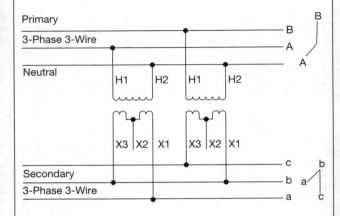

Open Wye-Delta

When operating wye-delta and one phase is disabled, service may be maintained at reduced load as shown. The neutral in this case must be connected to the neutral of the setup bank through a copper conductor. The system is unbalanced, electro-statically and electro-magnetically, so that telephone interference may be expected if the neutral is connected to ground. The useful capacity of the open delta open wye bank is 87% of the capacity of the installed transformers when the two units are identical.

THREE-PHASE TRANSFORMER CONNECTIONS *(cont.)*

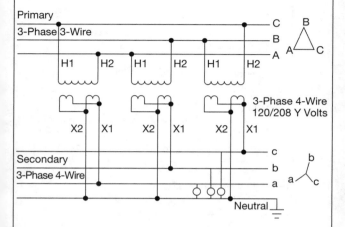

Delta-Wye for Lighting and Power

In the previous banks the single-phase lighting load is all on one phase resulting in unbalanced primary currents in any one bank. To eliminate this difficulty, the delta-wye system finds many uses. Here the neutral of the secondary three-phase system is grounded and the single-phase loads are connected between the different phase wires and the neutral while the three-phase loads are connected to the phase wires. Thus, the single-phase load can be balanced on three phases in each bank and banks may be paralleled if desired.

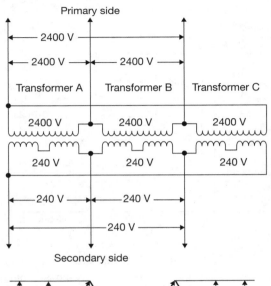

Primary side

2400 V

2400 V   2400 V

Transformer A   Transformer B   Transformer C

2400 V   2400 V   2400 V

240 V   240 V   240 V

240 V   240 V

240 V

Secondary side

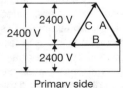

Primary side

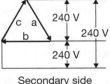

Secondary side

Delta-to-Delta Connection

In a delta-to-delta connection, the voltage of each transformer is equal to the 3φ line voltage and the current in each of the transformers is only 57.7% of the line current.

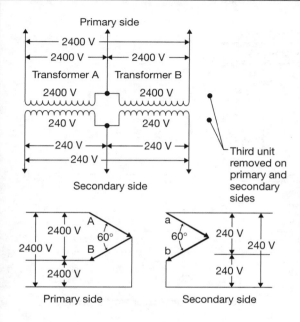

Primary side

2400 V

2400 V — 2400 V

Transformer A | Transformer B

2400 V | 2400 V

240 V | 240 V

240 V — 240 V

240 V

Secondary side

Third unit removed on primary and secondary sides

A
2400 V
60°
2400 V
B
2400 V

Primary side

a
60°
240 V
240 V
b
240 V

Secondary side

Open-Delta Connection

An open-delta connection enables continued operation if one 1ϕ transformer or one winding of a 3ϕ shell-type transformer in a delta-to-delta system becomes defective.

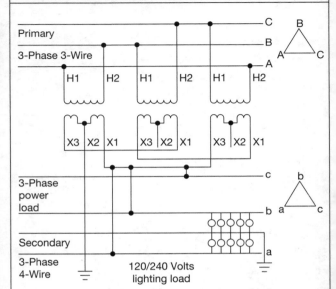

Delta-Delta for Power and Lighting

This connection is used to supply a small single-phase lighting load and three-phase power load simultaneously. As shown, the midtap of the secondary of one transformer is grounded. The small lighting load is connected across the transformer with the midtap and the ground wire common to both 120 V circuits. The single-phase lighting load reduces the available three-phase capacity. This requires special watt-hour metering.

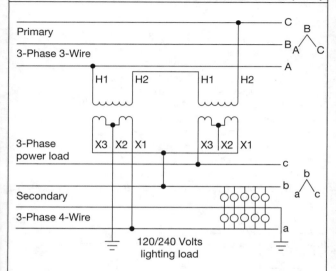

Primary

3-Phase 3-Wire

3-Phase power load

Secondary

3-Phase 4-Wire

120/240 Volts lighting load

Open-Delta for Lighting and Power

Where the secondary load is a combination of lighting and power, the open-delta connected bank is frequently used. This connection is used when the single-phase lighting load is large as compared with the power load. Here two different size transformers may be used with the lighting load connected across the larger rated unit.

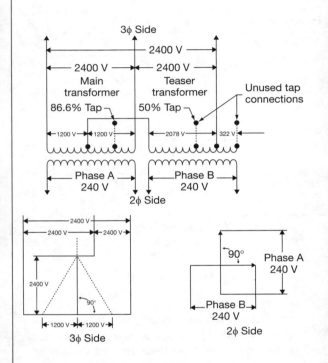

Scott Connection

Three-phase to 2φ or 2φ to 3φ transformation may be accomplished using the Scott connection.

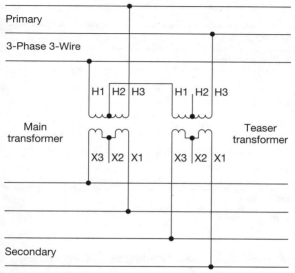

Scott Connected Three-Phase to Two-Phase

When two-phase power is required from a three-phase system, the Scott connection is used the most. The secondary may be three, four, or five wire. Special taps must be provided at 50% and 86.6% of normal primary voltage to make this connection.

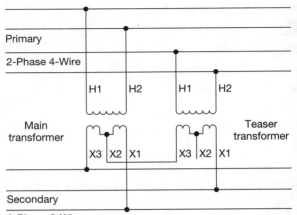

Primary

2-Phase 4-Wire

Main transformer

Teaser transformer

Secondary

3-Phase 3-Wire

Scott Connected Two-Phase to Three-Phase

If it should be necessary to supply three-phase power from a two-phase system, the Scott connection may be used again. The special taps must be provided on the secondary side, but the connection is similar to the three-phase to two-phase.

To obtain the Scott transformation without a special 86.6% tapped transformer, use one with 10% or two 5% taps to approximate the desired value. A small error of unbalance (overvoltage) occurs that requires care in application.

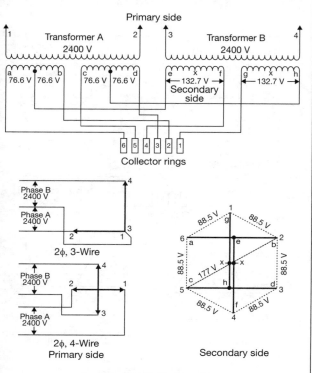

Double Scott Connection

Two 1ϕ transformers connected in a double Scott connection are used when operating a 6ϕ synchronous converter from a 2ϕ circuit.

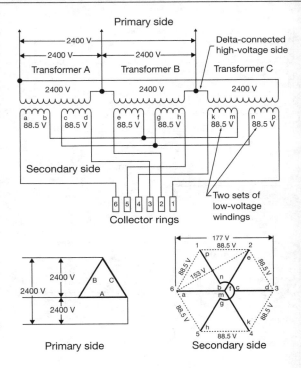

Double-Wye Connection

A double-wye connection requires two sets of low-voltage windings displaced 180° in phase with each other.

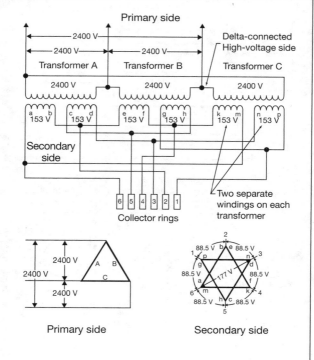

Primary side

Secondary side

Double-Delta Connection

A double-delta connection requires two separate low-voltage windings on each transformer.

THREE-PHASE TRANSFORMER CONNECTIONS (cont.)

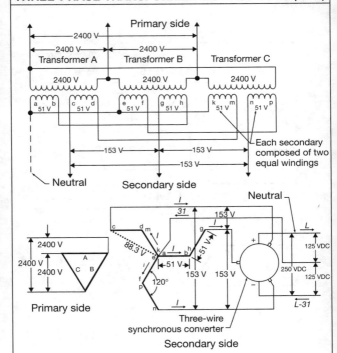

Primary side

Secondary side

Primary side

Secondary side

Three-wire synchronous converter

Delta-to-Interconnected Wye Connection

Synchronous converters are often connected to transformers connected delta-to-interconnected wye to eliminate the flux distortion in the transformer due to the unbalanced DC in the neutral of the 3-wire circuit flowing through the windings.

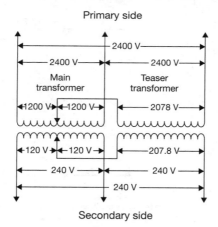

Primary side

Secondary side

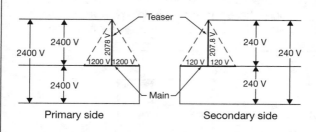

Primary side   Secondary side

T-to-T Connection

In a T-to-T connection, one of the units is the main transformer and is provided with a 50% voltage tap to which a teaser transformer is connected.

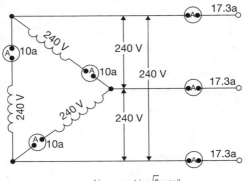

Line current is $\sqrt{3}$ × coil
current in a delta connection

Current and voltage values on a delta bank of three
single-phase transformer windings. A voltage of 240
volts and a current of 10 amperes are assumed.

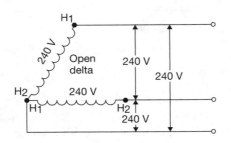

Two Transformers in an Open Delta Arrangement

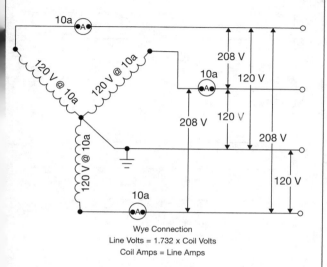

Wye Connection
Line Volts = 1.732 x Coil Volts
Coil Amps = Line Amps

Current and voltage values on a wye bank of three single-phase transformer windings. A voltage of 120 volts and a current of 10 amperes are assumed.

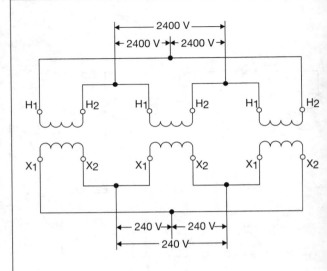

Delta-Delta

Three single-phase transformers connected in a delta-delta bank; the high side is connected to 2400 volts, three-phase, and the low side delivers 240 volts, three-phase.

CURRENT TRANSFORMER

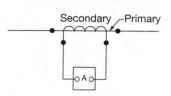

TESTING A TRANSFORMER FOR POLARITY

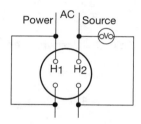

CURRENT-VOLTAGE RELATIONSHIP BETWEEN HIGH SIDE AND LOW SIDE OF A TRANSFORMER

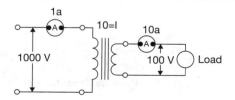

SPLIT-COIL TRANSFORMER AND AN ADDITIVE-POLARITY TRANSFORMER

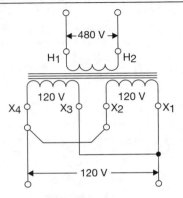

Split-Coil Transformer

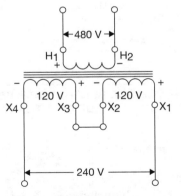

Additive-Polarity Transformer

SECONDARY TIES

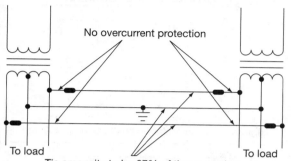

No overcurrent protection

Tie ampacity to be 67% of the secondary
current of the largest transformer.

LOADS CONNECTED BETWEEN
TRANSFORMER SUPPLY POINTS

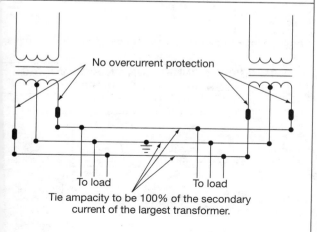

No overcurrent protection

To load   To load

Tie ampacity to be 100% of the secondary
current of the largest transformer.

PROHIBITED CONNECTIONS ON HIGH-VOLTAGE LIGHTING TRANSFORMERS

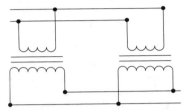

High-voltage secondaries shall not be paralleled.

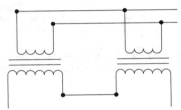

High-voltage secondaries shall not be connected in series.

PERMISSIBLE CONNECTION ON HIGH-VOLTAGE LIGHTING TRANSFORMERS

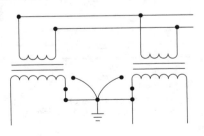

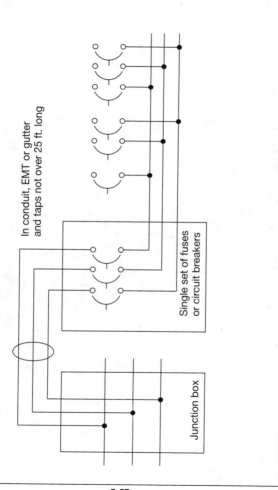

TAP CIRCUITS NOT OVER 25 FEET LONG

In conduit, EMT or gutter and taps not over 25 ft. long

Single set of fuses or circuit breakers

Junction box

5-37

TRANSFORMER FEED TAPS NOT OVER 25 FEET LONG

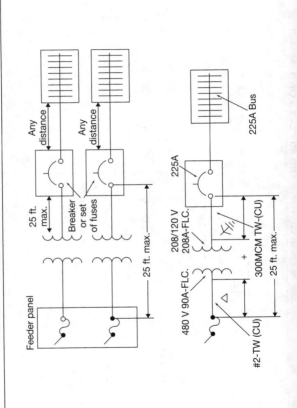

Feeder panel

Any distance

Any distance

25 ft. max.

Breaker or set of fuses

25 ft. max.

225A

225A Bus

208/120 V
208A-FLC.

300MCM TW-(CU)

25 ft. max.

480 V 90A-FLC.

#2-TW (CU)

AUTOTRANSFORMER

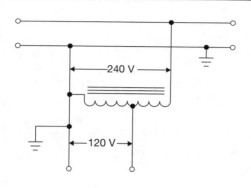

240 V

120 V

Buck
Voltage

Two hot
conductors

208 V

240 V

Two hot
conductors

Boost
Voltage

Line
voltage

0 V to line
voltage

Load

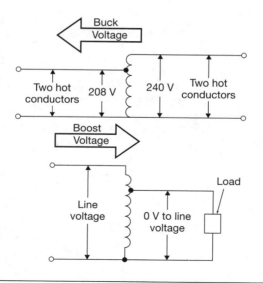

AUTOTRANSFORMER DIMMER CIRCUIT

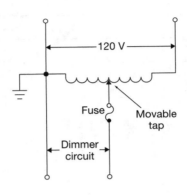

AUTOTRANSFORMER VOLTAGE BOOSTER

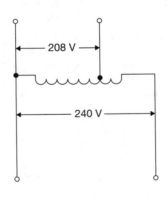

AUTOTRANSFORMER CONNECTIONS

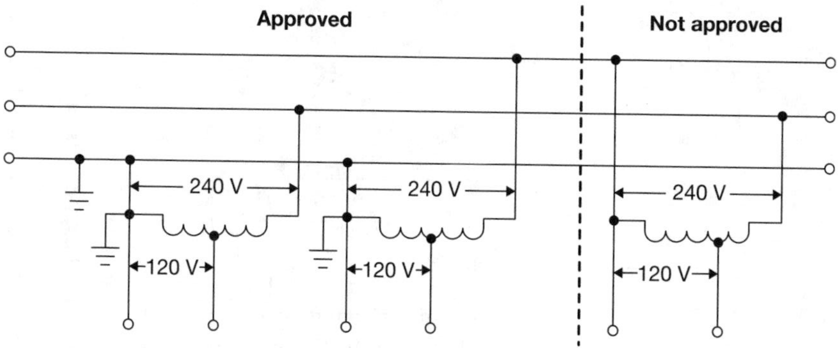

Approved

240 V
120 V

240 V
120 V

Not approved

240 V
120 V

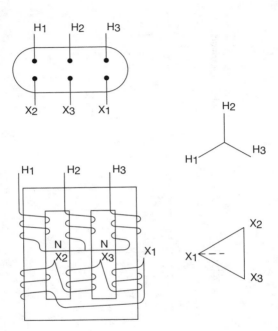

Terminal markings for a star-delta connected three-phase transformer having additive polarity, 30° angular displacement, and standard phase rotation.

DELTA-DELTA CONNECTED

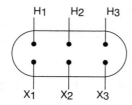

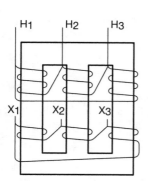

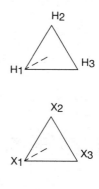

Terminal markings for a delta-delta connected three-phase transformer having subtractive polarity, 0° phase displacement, and standard phase rotation.

STAR-STAR CONNECTED

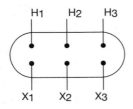

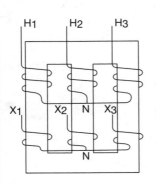

Terminal markings for a star-star connected three-phase transformer having subtractive polarity, 0° phase displacement, and standard phase rotation.

CHAPTER 6
Power Distribution

Electrical power distribution systems are composed of three main parts — the electric service, distribution equipment, and feeder circuits. The initial feed of power into a building comes through the electrical service (power provided by a utility company). The service power is fed through service panels, which contain appropriate overcurrent protection devices. From there, power is distributed to additional overcurrent protected panels through feeder circuits. In most cases, individual conductors in raceways are used for these circuits, although busways are frequently used as well.

It is important that electrical services be properly installed because the service conductors may be effectively unfused. For example, the typical service conductors are often fed directly from utility lines that are fused at several thousand amperes. In this case, the service conductors have so high a level of available current, that they would melt and burn long before the overcurrent device will interrupt the current. Utility companies work at avoiding problems like this, but the problem is still widespread.

Feeders are circuits which distribute fairly large quantities of power between distribution (service) panels and branch-circuit panels. The physical routing of feeders is a very important consideration on the job site. Since feeders can easily cost $50 to $150 per foot, the length of a run should be minimized wherever possible.

MULTIWIRE SYSTEM VOLTAGES

120/208 V, 3φ, 4-wire wye

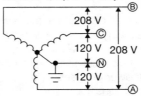

A to B = 208 V
B to C = 208 V
A to N = 120 V
C to N = 120 V

277/480 V, 3φ, 4-wire wye

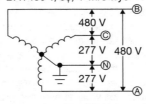

A to B = 480 V
B to C = 480 V
A to N = 277 V
C to N = 277 V

Wye-Connected

120/240 V, 3φ, 4-wire delta

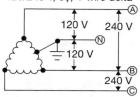

A to B = 240 V
B to C = 240 V
A to N = 120 V
B to N = 120 V
C to N = Not used

480 V, 3φ, 3-wire delta

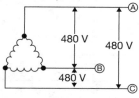

A to B = 480 V
B to C = 480 V
A to C = 480 V

Delta-Connected

4-WIRE CIRCUITS

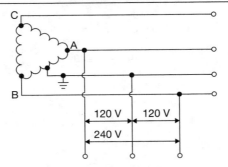

One type of multiwire circuit from a 4-wire delta system.

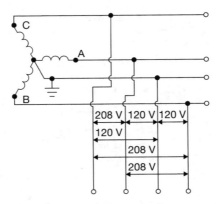

Multiwire circuit from a 4-wire wye system.

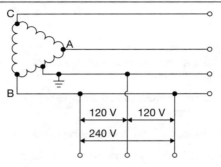

Not a multiwire circuit from a 4-wire delta system.

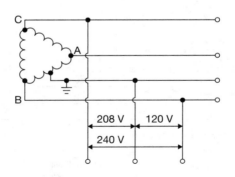

Not a multiwire circuit from a 4-wire delta system.

HIGH-LEG OF 4-WIRE DELTA SYSTEM

- Bus bars require phase arrangement top to bottom

- Bus bars require phase arrangement left to right

- Grounded conductors shall be white

- Phase B shall be high-leg and identified

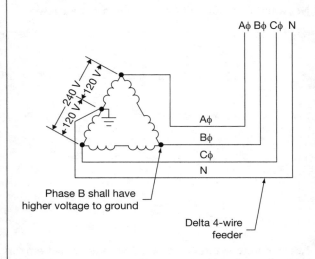

Phase B shall have higher voltage to ground

Delta 4-wire feeder

PHASE ARRANGEMENT FOR
THREE-PHASE BUS BARS

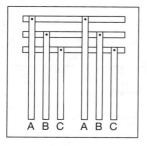

Phase arrangement of
3φ buses shall be A, B, C
from front to back,
top to bottom, and
left to right

Front view

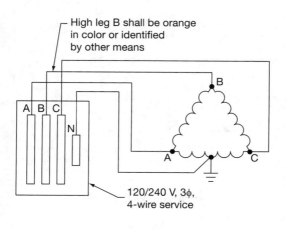

High leg B shall be orange
in color or identified
by other means

A B C

B

N

A

C

120/240 V, 3φ,
4-wire service

3-WIRE CIRCUITS

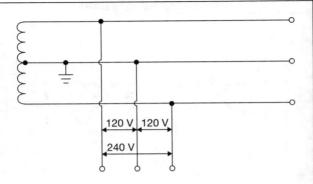

3-wire, 120/240 V, multiwire circuit.

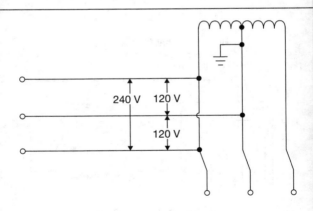

<u>Not</u> a multiwire circuit.

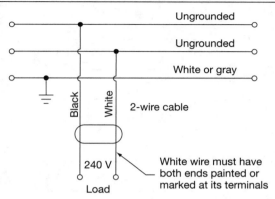

Ungrounded

Ungrounded

White or gray

Black

White

2-wire cable

240 V

Load

White wire must have both ends painted or marked at its terminals

**2-wire cable connected
to the two hot wires of a 3-wire circuit.**

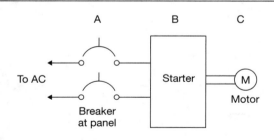

A   B   C

To AC

Starter

M

Motor

Breaker
at panel

**Typical motor circuit. The branch
circuit extends from point A to point C.**

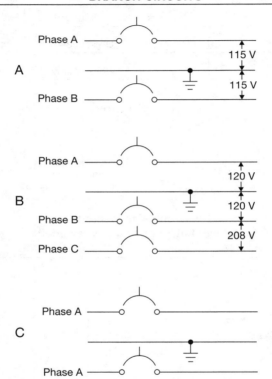

BRANCH CIRCUITS

A

Phase A

115 V

115 V

Phase B

B

Phase A

120 V

120 V

Phase B

208 V

Phase C

C

Phase A

Phase A

**Variations of a multiwire branch circuit.
<u>Circuit C is not</u> a multiwire branch circuit
because it utilizes two wires from the same
phase in conjunction with the neutral conductor.**

BRANCH CIRCUIT GROUNDING

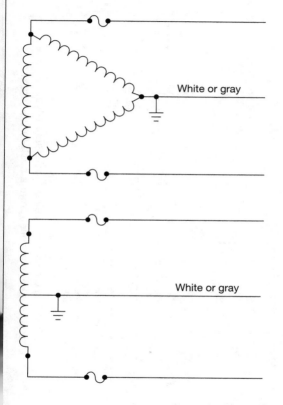

White or gray

White or gray

Grounded conductor in a branch circuit.

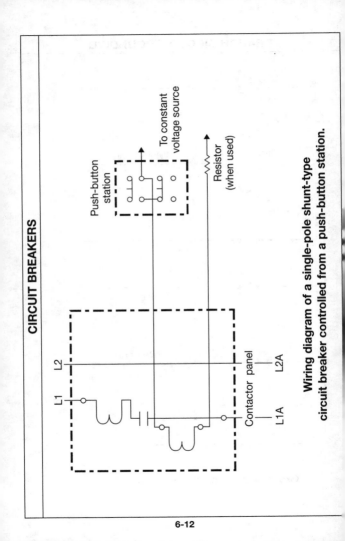

Wiring diagram of a single-pole shunt-type circuit breaker controlled from a push-button station.

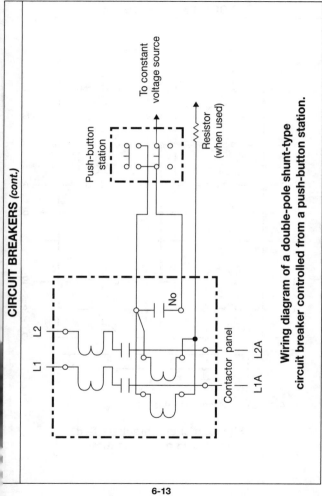

**Wiring diagram of a double-pole shunt-type
circuit breaker controlled from a push-button station.**

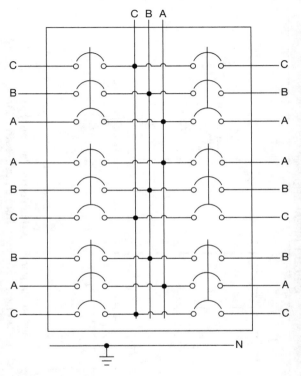

A=Black   B=Red   C=Blue

**Eighteen circuit breakers tied
together in groups of three.**

OVERCURRENT PROTECTION

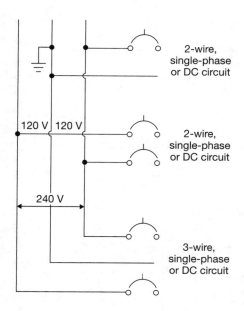

2-wire,
single-phase
or DC circuit

120 V | 120 V

2-wire,
single-phase
or DC circuit

240 V

3-wire,
single-phase
or DC circuit

**Overcurrent protection for a
3-wire, single-phase system.**

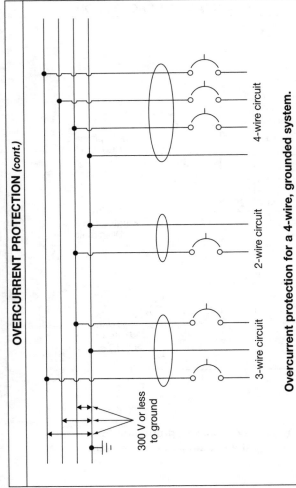

300 V or less to ground

3-wire circuit

2-wire circuit

4-wire circuit

Overcurrent protection for a 4-wire, grounded system.

CURRENT AND VOLTAGE
TRANSFORMER CONNECTIONS

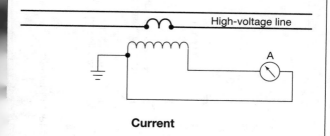

Current

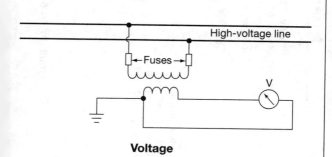

Voltage

TAP CIRCUIT

Primary of transformer
protected as per NEC article 450

Secondary of transformer

Enclosed in
raceway

Not less than ampere
rating of buses, etc.

10 ft. max.
including bus

Not less than the
combined loads on
the circuits supplied
by the tap conductors

Tap circuit not to exceed 10 feet in length.

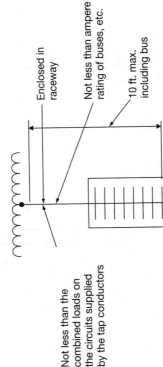

MINIMUM SERVICE-DROP CLEARANCE

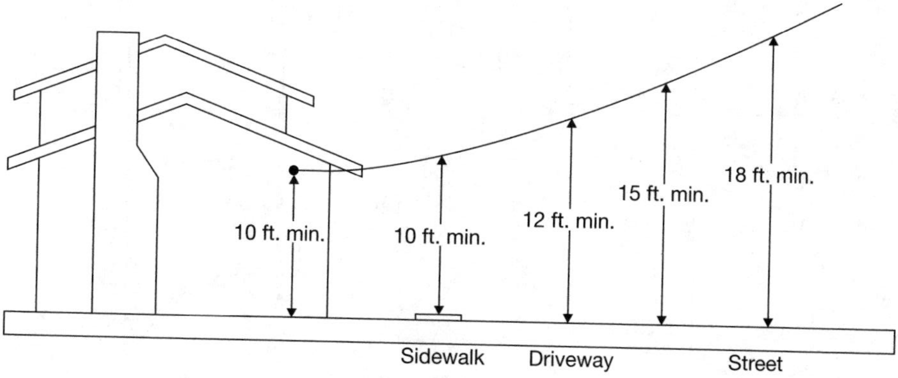

10 ft. min.

10 ft. min.

12 ft. min.

15 ft. min.

18 ft. min.

Sidewalk   Driveway   Street

6-19

SERVICE DROP ATTACHED TO A BUILDING OR OTHER STRUCTURE

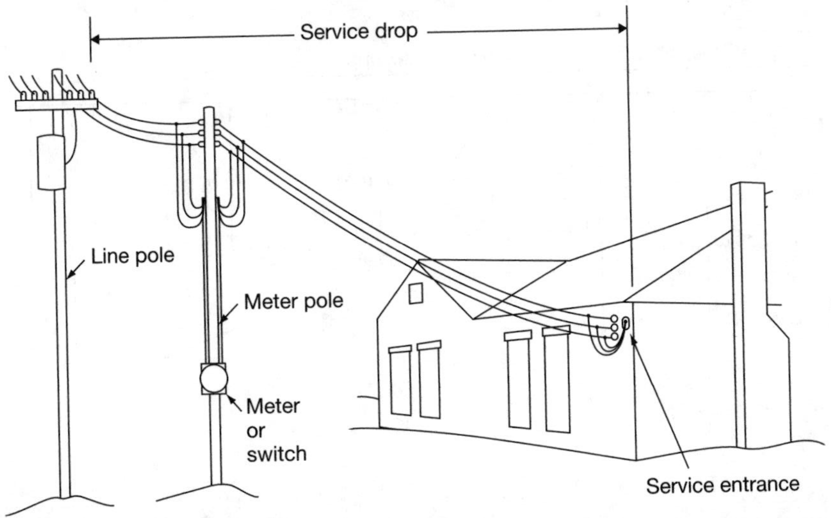

Service entrance

Service drop

Meter pole

Meter or switch

Line pole

6-20

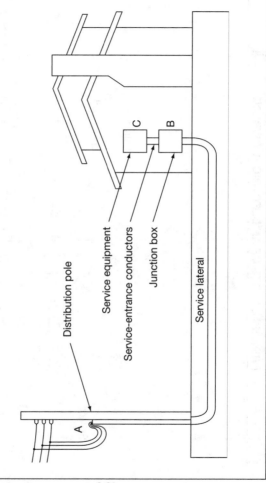

SERVICE LATERAL EXTENDING FROM POINT A TO POINT B. THE SERVICE ENTRANCE IS FROM POINT B TO POINT C.

Distribution pole

Service equipment

Service-entrance conductors

Junction box

Service lateral

C

B

A

6-21

PRINCIPAL PARTS OF AN ELECTRICAL SERVICE

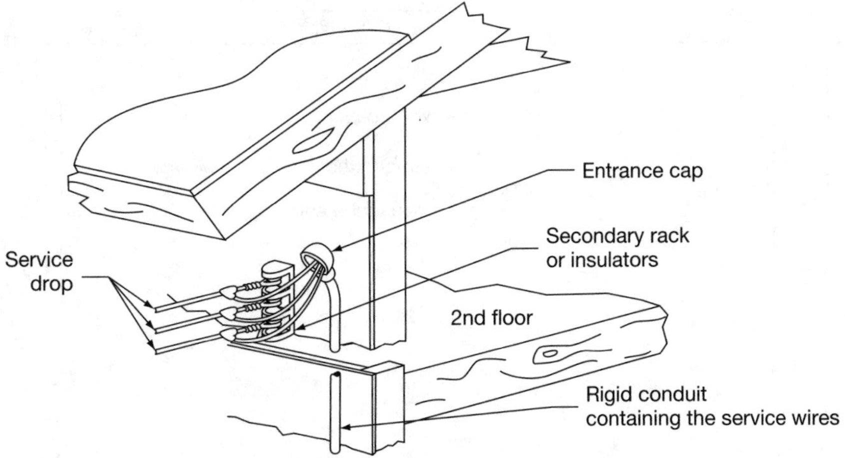

Entrance cap

Secondary rack
or insulators

2nd floor

Rigid conduit
containing the service wires

Service
drop

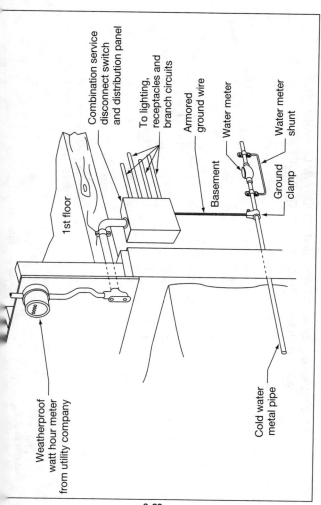

Combination service
disconnect switch
and distribution panel

To lighting,
receptacles and
branch circuits

Armored
ground wire

Water meter

Basement

1st floor

Ground
clamp

Water meter shunt

Weatherproof
watt hour meter
from utility company

Cold water
metal pipe

6-23

UNDERGROUND SERVICE CONDUIT TO SIDEWALK HAND HOLE
AND UNDERGROUND SERVICE CONDUCTORS

Duct for utility power lines

Gravel

Drain

Bushing

Galvanized rigid conduit may
be buried directly in some types of soil

Power company
sidewalk hand hole

Basement

Concrete wall

Bushing and
locknut

Service switch

1/4" air space
between wall
suface and
service switch

6-24

BONDING FLEXIBLE METAL CONDUIT IN A SERVICE ENTRANCE

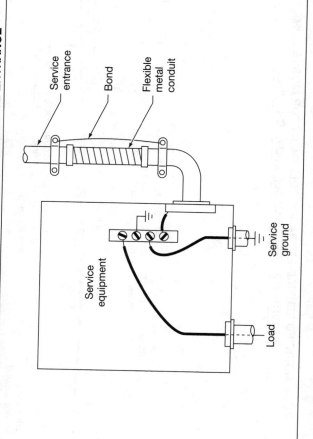

Service entrance

Bond

Flexible metal conduit

Service ground

Service equipment

Load

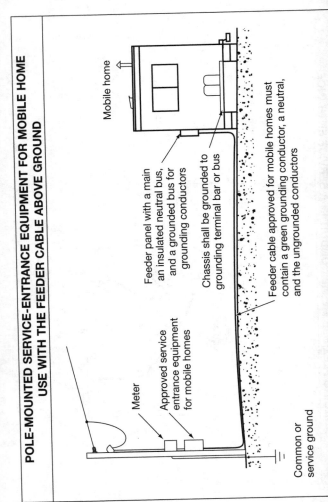

POLE-MOUNTED SERVICE-ENTRANCE EQUIPMENT FOR MOBILE HOME
USE WITH THE FEEDER CABLE ABOVE GROUND

Mobile home

Feeder panel with a main
an insulated neutral bus,
and a grounded bus for
grounding conductors

Chassis shall be grounded to
grounding terminal bar or bus

Feeder cable approved for mobile homes must
contain a green grounding conductor, a neutral,
and the ungrounded conductors

Meter

Approved service
entrance equipment
for mobile homes

Common or
service ground

6-26

UNDERGROUND SERVICE LATERAL FOR USE WITH MOBILE HOME

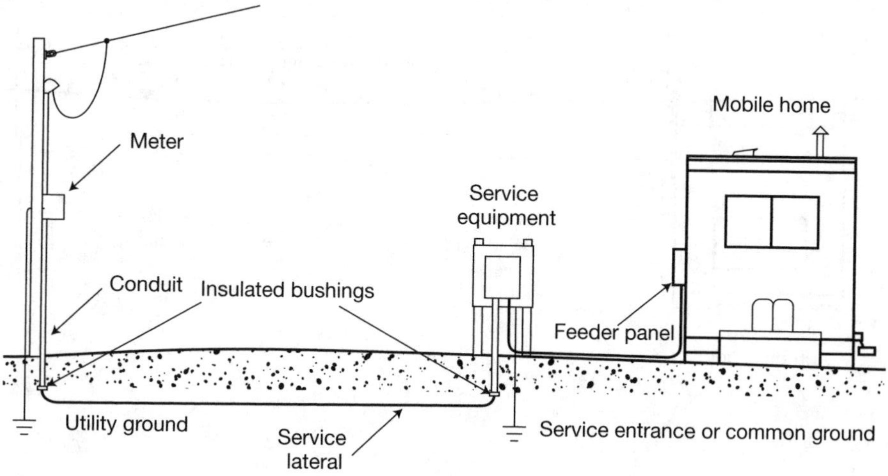

Mobile home
Meter
Service
equipment
Conduit
Insulated bushings
Feeder panel
Utility ground
Service
lateral
Service entrance or common ground

POLE-MOUNTED SERVICE-ENTRANCE EQUIPMENT FOR MOBILE HOME
USE WITH THE FEEDER CABLE BURIED

Mobile home

Feeder panel

Conduit

Insulated bushings

Feeder-circuit cable must contain a neutral,
a grounding conductor, and two ungrounded conductors

Meter

Service entrance
equipment

Common
ground

AN OVERHEAD FEEDER-CABLE INSTALLATION TO SUPPLY POWER TO A MOBILE HOME

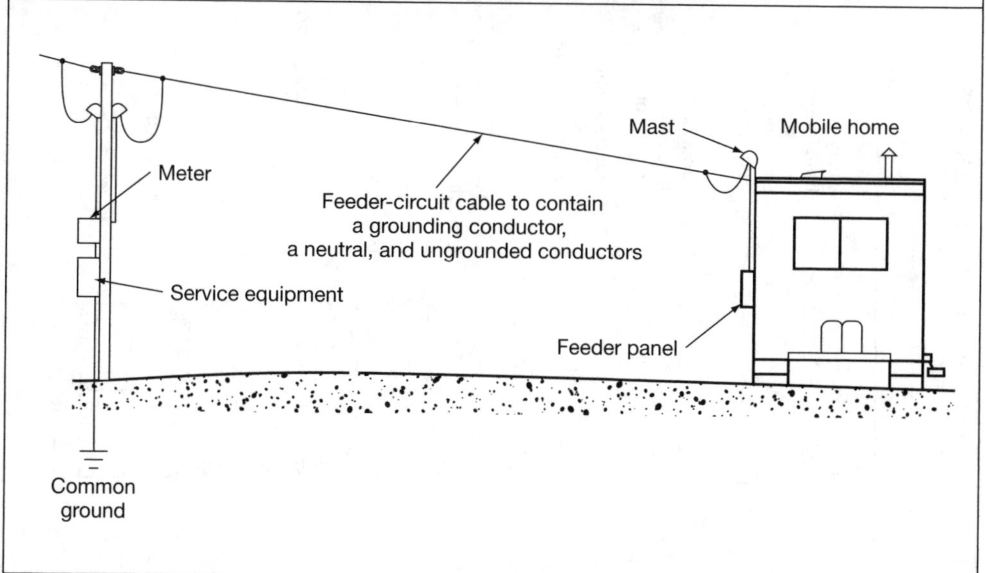

Mobile home

Mast

Feeder panel

Feeder-circuit cable to contain
a grounding conductor,
a neutral, and ungrounded conductors

Service equipment

Meter

Common
ground

6-29

120/240 V, 1φ, 3-WIRE SERVICE

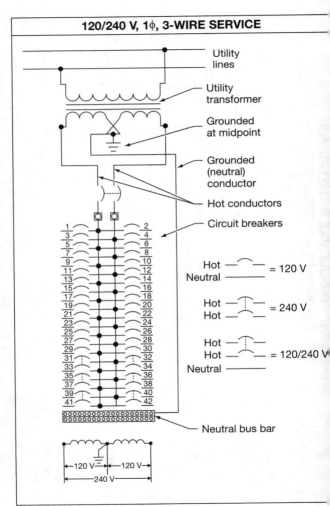

Utility lines

Utility transformer

Grounded at midpoint

Grounded (neutral) conductor

Hot conductors

Circuit breakers

Hot ⌒ Neutral ___ = 120 V

Hot ⌒ Hot ⌒ = 240 V

Hot ⌒ Hot ⌒ Neutral ___ = 120/240 V

Neutral bus bar

← 120 V → ← 120 V →

← 240 V →

6-30

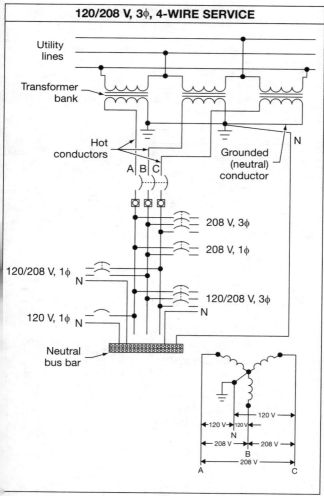

120/208 V, 3φ, 4-WIRE SERVICE

Utility lines

Transformer bank

Hot conductors

A B C

Grounded (neutral) conductor

N

208 V, 3φ

208 V, 1φ

120/208 V, 1φ

N

120/208 V, 3φ

N

120 V, 1φ

N

Neutral bus bar

120 V
120 V
120 V
N
120 V
208 V
208 V
B
208 V
A
C

6-31

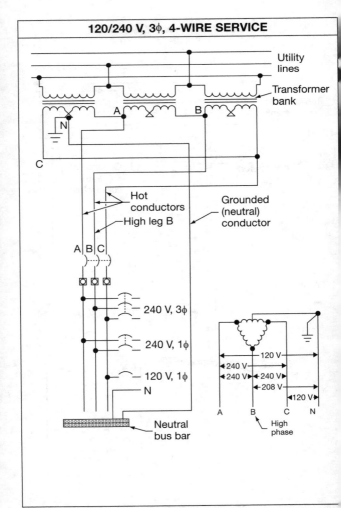

120/240 V, 3φ, 4-WIRE SERVICE

Utility lines

Transformer bank

A

N

B

C

Hot conductors

High leg B

Grounded (neutral) conductor

A B C

240 V, 3φ

240 V, 1φ

120 V, 1φ

N

Neutral bus bar

120 V

240 V

240 V

240 V

208 V

120 V

A

B
High phase

C

N

6-32

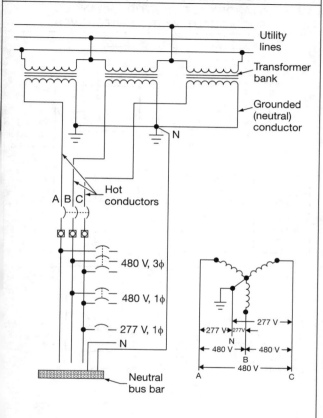

277/480 V, 3φ, 4-WIRE SERVICE

Utility lines

Transformer bank

Grounded (neutral) conductor

N

Hot conductors

A B C

480 V, 3φ

480 V, 1φ

277 V, 1φ

N

Neutral bus bar

277 V

277 V

277 V

N

480 V

480 V

480 V

A B C

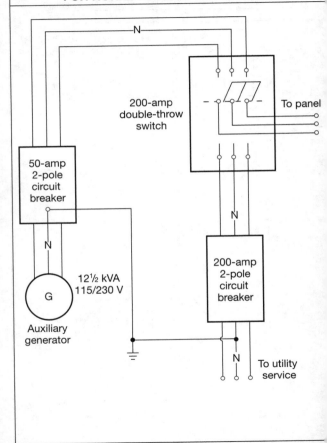

200-AMPERE SERVICE WITH A 12½ kVA STANDBY ALTERNATOR ARRANGED FOR NONAUTOMATIC SWITCHOVER

N

200-amp double-throw switch

To panel

50-amp 2-pole circuit breaker

N

12½ kVA 115/230 V

G

Auxiliary generator

N

200-amp 2-pole circuit breaker

N

To utility service

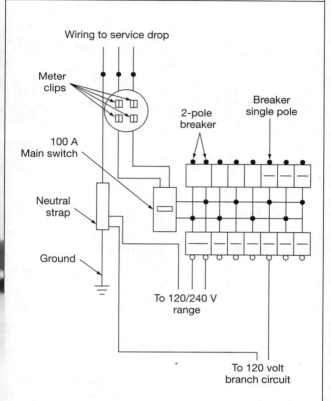

METER DIAGRAMS

Wiring to service drop

Meter clips

2-pole breaker

Breaker single pole

100 A Main switch

Neutral strap

Ground

To 120/240 V range

To 120 volt branch circuit

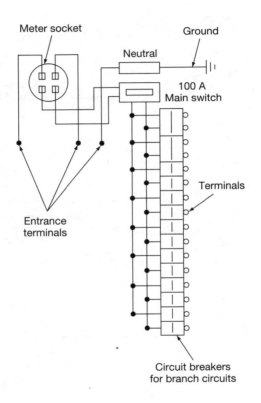

Meter socket

Ground

Neutral

100 A
Main switch

Entrance
terminals

Terminals

Circuit breakers
for branch circuits

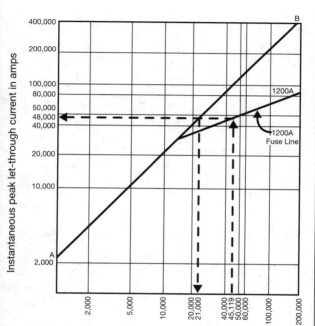

LET-THROUGH CHART FOR A 1200A CLASS L FUSE

Instantaneous peak let-through current in amps

400,000
200,000

100,000
80,000

50,000
48,000
40,000

20,000

10,000

A
2,000

B

1200A

1200A
Fuse Line

Prospective short-circuit current—symmetrical RMS amps

2,000 5,000 10,000 20,000 21,000 40,000 45,119 50,000 60,000 100,000 200,000

SINGLE LOW-TENSION, DOUBLE HIGH-TENSION BUS

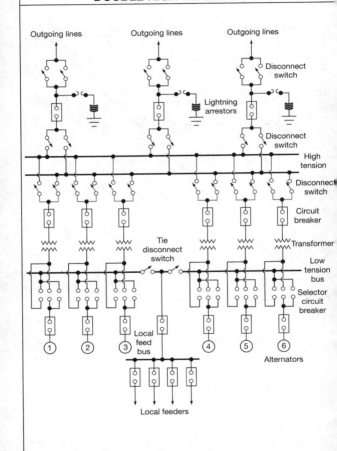

6-38

SINGLE HIGH-TENSION BUS

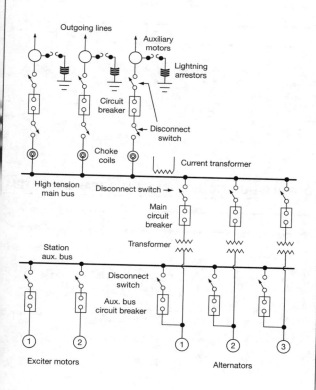

Outgoing lines

Auxiliary motors

Lightning arrestors

Circuit breaker

Disconnect switch

Choke coils

Current transformer

High tension main bus

Disconnect switch →

Main circuit breaker

Transformer

Station aux. bus

Disconnect switch

Aux. bus circuit breaker

① ②

Exciter motors

① ② ③

Alternators

DOUBLE-BUS SYSTEM WITH THE TIE BUS IN DOTTED LINE

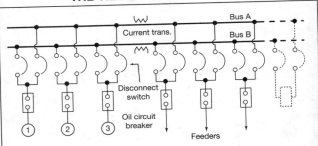

Bus A

Bus B

Current trans.

Disconnect switch

Oil circuit breaker

Feeders

① ② ③

DOUBLE-BUS, DOUBLE-CIRCUIT BREAKER SYSTEM

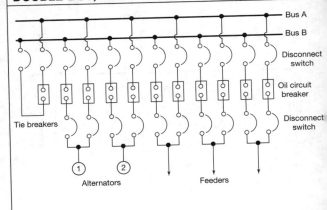

Bus A

Bus B

Disconnect switch

Oil circuit breaker

Disconnect switch

Tie breakers

Alternators ① ②

Feeders

RING-BUS SYSTEM

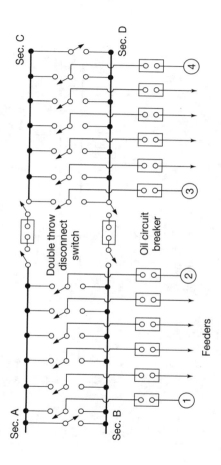

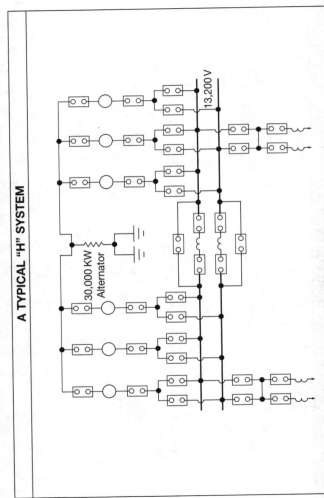

A TYPICAL "H" SYSTEM

30,000 KW Alternator

13,200 V

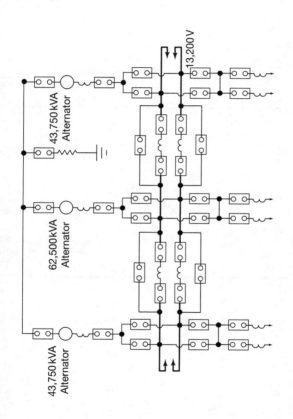

SYSTEM USING SINGLE LOW- AND SINGLE HIGH-TENSION BUS

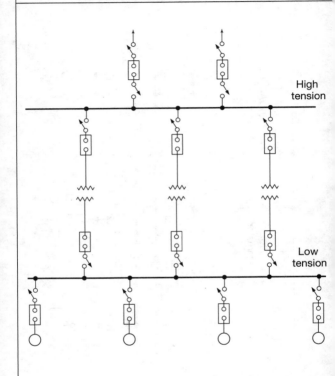

BUS SYSTEM USING DOUBLE BUSES AND DOUBLE CIRCUIT BREAKERS

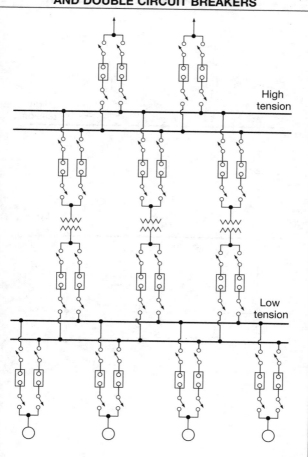

High tension

Low tension

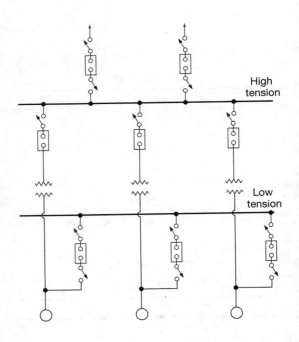

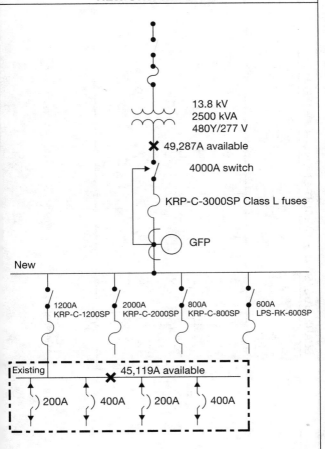

OLD SWITCHBOARD BEING FED FROM NEW SWITCHBOARD

13.8 kV
2500 kVA
480Y/277 V

49,287A available

4000A switch

KRP-C-3000SP Class L fuses

GFP

New

1200A
KRP-C-1200SP

2000A
KRP-C-2000SP

800A
KRP-C-800SP

600A
LPS-RK-600SP

Existing   45,119A available

200A   400A   200A   400A

SPARE-BUS, SPARE-CIRCUIT-BREAKER SYSTEM

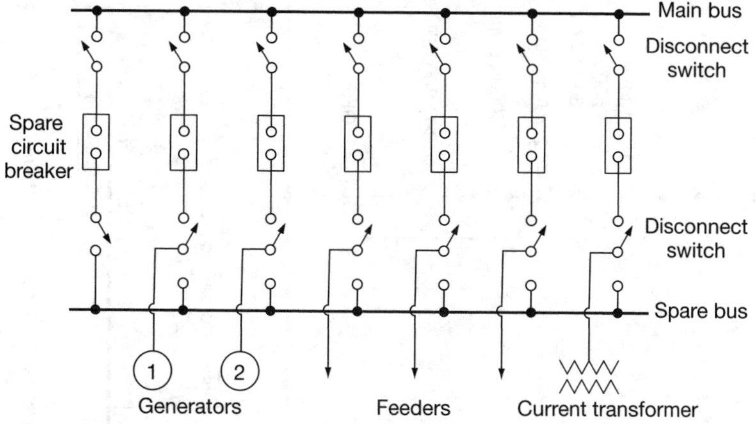

Main bus
Disconnect switch
Disconnect switch
Spare bus
Current transformer
Feeders
Generators
Spare circuit breaker

1

2

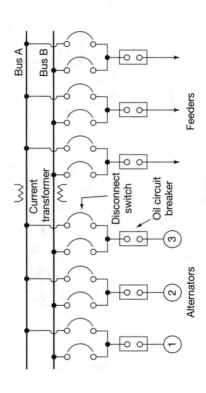

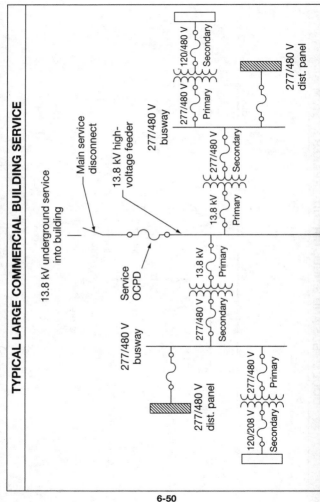

TYPICAL LARGE COMMERCIAL BUILDING SERVICE

13.8 kV underground service into building

Main service disconnect

Service OCPD

13.8 kV high-voltage feeder

277/480 V busway

277/480 V dist. panel

120/480 V Secondary

277/480 V Primary

277/480 V Secondary

13.8 kV Primary

13.8 kV Primary

277/480 V Secondary

277/480 V busway

277/480 V dist. panel

120/208 V Secondary

277/480 V Primary

6-50

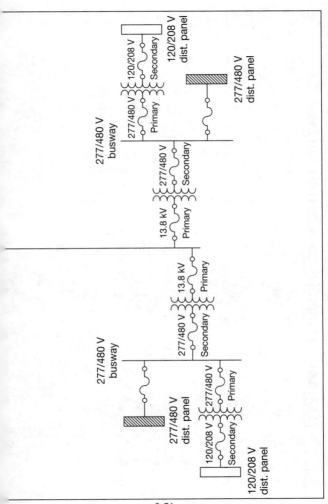

6-51

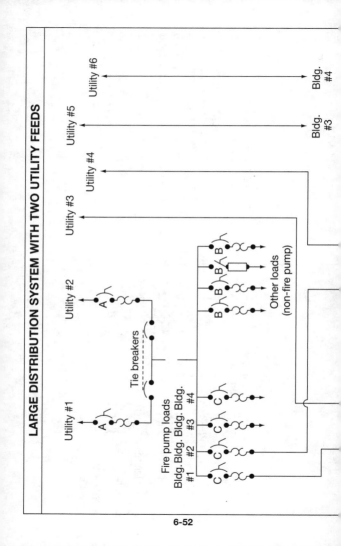

LARGE DISTRIBUTION SYSTEM WITH TWO UTILITY FEEDS

Utility #6

Utility #5

Utility #4

Utility #3

Utility #2

Utility #1

Bldg. #4

Bldg. #3

Tie breakers

Other loads (non-fire pump)

Fire pump loads
Bldg. Bldg. Bldg. Bldg.
#1   #2   #3   #4

6-52

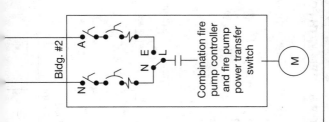

LARGE DISTRIBUTION SYSTEM WITH FOUR UTILITY FEEDS

Utility #1   Utility #2   Utility #3   Utility #4

Tie breakers   Set 1   Set 2   Tie breakers

Fire pump loads
Bldg. Bldg. Bldg. Bldg.
#1   #2   #3   #4

Other loads
(non-fire pump)

Fire pump loads
Bldg. Bldg. Bldg. Bldg.
#1   #2   #3   #4

Other loads
(non-fire pump)

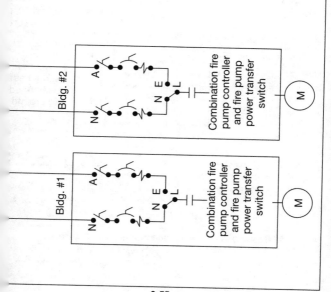

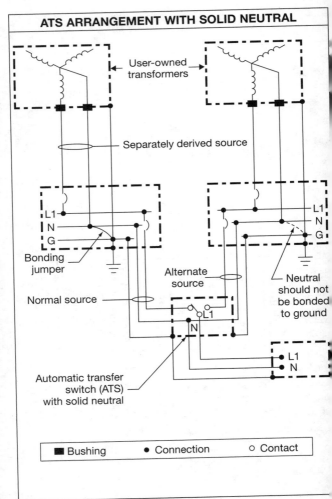

ATS ARRANGEMENT WITH SOLID NEUTRAL

User-owned transformers

Separately derived source

L1
N
G

Bonding jumper

L1
N
G

Neutral should not be bonded to ground

Alternate source

Normal source

Automatic transfer switch (ATS) with solid neutral

L1
N

L1
N

■ Bushing   ● Connection   ○ Contact

6-56

ATS ARRANGEMENT WITH SWITCHED-NEUTRAL

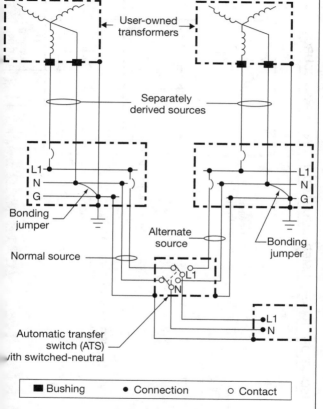

**Switched neutral creates a
separately derived system for each transformer.**

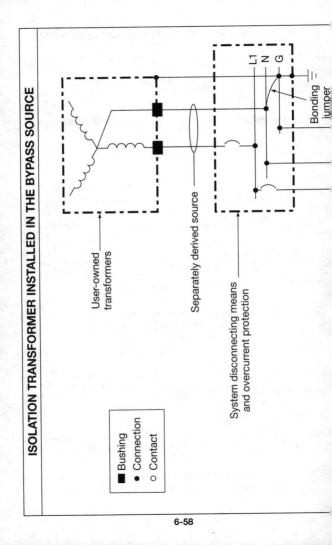

ISOLATION TRANSFORMER INSTALLED IN THE BYPASS SOURCE

User-owned transformers

Separately derived source

System disconnecting means and overcurrent protection

L1
N
G

Bonding jumper

■ Bushing
● Connection
○ Contact

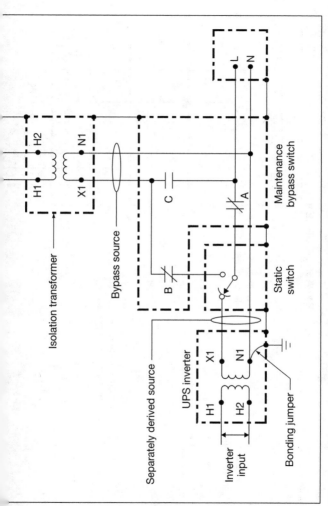

6-59

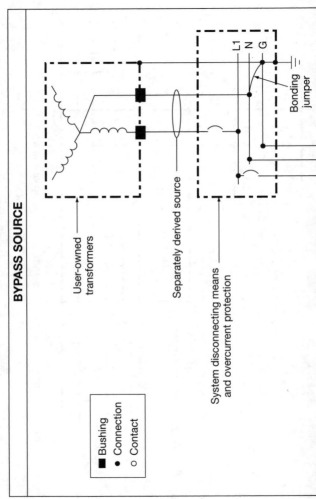

BYPASS SOURCE

User-owned transformers

Separately derived source

System disconnecting means and overcurrent protection

L1
N
G

Bonding jumper

■ Bushing
● Connection
○ Contact

6-60